GREAT ESCAPES

GREAT ESCAPES

**Alcatraz, the Berlin Wall, Colditz, Devil's Island
and 20 other stories of daring, audacity and ingenuity**

IAN CROFTON

Contents

Introduction

To find our freedom threatened or denied, to be made a captive – whether as prison inmate, slave or victim of oppression – erodes our sense of ourselves as autonomous individuals, so diminishing what it means to us to be human. But it is only when we are constrained by the will of others, prevented from fulfilling our own destiny, that we realize the true value of liberty.

Any man or woman who strives against all odds to regain or maintain their freedom compels our attention. Some of the oldest stories in the world involve the hero escaping from captivity or evading some deadly peril through a combination of courage, resolve and cunning. The hero who is vulnerable, persecuted or threatened draws out our sympathies more than the great warrior who wins out simply by brute force of arms.

The first tale in this book is the ancient Greek legend of Daedalus, who made wings for himself and his son Icarus so that they might escape from the clutches of King Minos. Locked within the legend is a memory of the ancient Minoans, a bull-worshipping civilization that flourished on the Mediterranean island of Crete in the 3rd millennium BC. Almost as old – perhaps originating in the Mycenean era of the 2nd millennium BC – are the stories of the guileful Greek king Odysseus as he wanders around the Mediterranean on his long way back from the Trojan War. Among his many adventures are a number of escapes – from the deadly lure of the Sirens, from the many-headed monster Scylla, from the whirlpool Charybdis. Most memorable is his escape from Polyphemus, the one-eyed Cyclops, in whose cave he and his men are trapped when the giant returns from tending his flocks and blocks the entrance with a rock. Disregarding the laws of hospitality, Polyphemus picks up two of the Greeks and dashes their brains out on the floor before dismembering and devouring them – guts, flesh, bones and all. The ever-crafty Odysseus knows that if he kills Polyphemus he and his men will never be able to move the rock blocking the entrance, so he tells the giant his name is Outis, Nobody, then plies him with wine until he falls into a stupor. Once the their captor is unconscious, the Greeks heat a stake in the fire then drive it into the giant's single eye. As Polyphemus screams in agony, his fellow Cyclops gather round outside the door and demand to know the matter. 'Nobody is killing me!' he yells – so the other giants stump off, telling him not to make such a fuss if nobody is hurting him. In his pain and frenzy Polyphemus removes the rock and squats by the entrance, hoping to catch the Greeks and kill them should they try to sneak past. But Odysseus gets his men to hang onto the undersides of the giant's rams, and as the flocks trot out of the cave Polyphemus feels their backs but not their bellies – and so Odysseus and his men make good their escape.

The best escape stories are full of such tricks of concealment, subterfuge and disguise. Mary Queen of Scots' exit from Lochleven Castle was engineered by the wily page boy 'Little Willie' Douglas while seemingly engaged in drunken frolics in honour of May Day. The Cockney rascal Jack Sheppard showed all the lock-picking skills of a

Houdini in making his four escapes from jail in 1724, while 30 years later Casanova persuaded his treacherous if gullible cell mate that when his fellow escaper broke through the ceiling of their cell it was in fact a visitation by an angel. Bonnie Prince Charlie dressed himself up as an Irish serving maid before escaping across the sea to Skye, while in 1864 John Bray of the 1st New Jersey Cavalry was able to walk out of a Confederate prison in the uniform of a Confederate officer.

Some of the most famous escape stories are legacies of the Second World War. Via books and films, the escapades at Colditz and the tunnels out of Stalag Luft III have become part of our collective memory – in Britain, for example, no Christmas goes by without *The Great Escape* being shown on television. The fact that the film takes liberties with many of the details of the real escape does not detract from its appeal. And, contrary to common Hollywood practice, it does not substitute a happy ending for the brutal truth that the Gestapo murdered 50 of the escapers in cold blood.

Not all the stories in this book involve escapes from jails or prison camps. During the Second World War, supported by networks of courageous civilians, many Allied airmen shot down over Nazi-occupied Europe managed to evade capture altogether – as did one-third of a million Allied troops at Dunkirk in 1940. All too few European Jews survived the Holocaust unleashed by Hitler, but one such was Leo Bretholz, who spent six years on the run and avoided almost certain death by breaking out of the train taking him to Auschwitz – just one of a remarkable series of escapes.

Some men and women willingly put themselves in perilous situations, pitting themselves against the challenges of the natural, rather than the human, world. Exploring unknown continents, sailing across the oceans, climbing the highest mountains – all these endeavours have generated extraordinary tales of courage and endurance as the protagonists battle their way out of danger. Such stories of survival – Shackleton's escape from the Antarctic to South Georgia, Captain Bligh's 3000-mile voyage across the Pacific in an open boat, the return of the damaged *Apollo 13* from space – provide more than enough material for an entirely separate book, but in the present volume there is a flavour of such tales, in the form of the terrible retreat through a week-long storm by seven alpinists attempting to make the first ascent of one of the 'last great problems' on Mont Blanc, the highest mountain of the Alps.

That story ended in tragedy, but not all such endeavours end badly. One of the most uplifting stories to come out of the Second World War, retold here, is that of three Italian prisoners-of-war held in a camp in British East Africa, in sight of Mount Kenya. They determine to escape, not with any idea of carrying on the war, but with the sole intention of climbing that distant peak. War and imprisonment may crush people's spirits, but they can also fire them to transcend their physical confines and soar, as Daedalus did millennia before, flying high above the waves towards life and freedom.

Ian Crofton

FLIGHT FROM CRETE

Daedalus and Icarus take to the air

Daedalus, master artificer of Athens whose veins ran with the blood of kings, found pride but no solace in his craft. Pride made him kill his sister's son, abet a queen in her unnatural lusts, soar like a god through the sky to flee a tyrant's wrath. But in so soaring he lost the thing he loved, his son Icarus, who flew beyond him, above him, too close to the sun, and fell.

Daedalus – the very name means 'Ingenious' –was credited by the ancients with all sorts of cleverness. Pliny claimed he devised the techniques and tools of carpentry – the saw, the axe, the plumb line, the drill. Philostratus said he was the first to make statues that gave promise of motion. Others claimed he made the first sails, so ships could skim across the sea. Around the Mediterranean Daedalus was said to have designed many great buildings, from the temple of Ptah in Memphis to the magnificent shrine of Apollo at Cumae. 'And you too,' Virgil apostrophizes Icarus in the *Aeneid*, 'would have had a great part in this splendid work, but for Daedalus' grief. Twice he tried to shape your fall in gold, and twice his hands, a father's hands, dropped helpless.'

Birds, bulls and monsters

The Athenians claimed the man they called *Daidalos* as one of their own. He was, they said, the grandson or great-grandson of King Erechtheus, and his father was Metion, 'the knowledgeable one', or Eupalamus, 'the skilful one'. Daedalus was already established as a great craftsman when he took his nephew Perdix under his wing as his apprentice. The youth soon proved an even greater craftsman than his uncle, inventing the potter's wheel, compasses for drawing perfect circles, and – taking inspiration from the backbone of a fish or the teeth in the jaws of a snake – the iron saw. Daedalus, in his jealousy of his nephew, flung him from the cliffs of the Acropolis – but before he hit the ground and certain death, the goddess Athena, taking pity on the youth, turned him into a partridge, which, in Latin, bears his name – *perdix*. This bird, recalling that awful fall, to this day flies low over the fresh-cut corn and makes its nest not in trees or on cliffs, but on the ground.

> Such was the work, so intricate the place,
> That scarce the workman all its turns cou'd trace;
> And Daedalus was puzzled how to find
> The secret ways of what himself design'd.

Ovid, *Metamorphoses*, Book 8, describes the Labyrinth; translated by Sir Samuel Garth, John Dryden, et al.

The court of the Areopagus sent Daedalus into exile for his crime, and so the master artificer came to Crete. Here he found not all was well with the family of King Minos. The problem was the bulls. Minos himself had been fathered on his

---

OPPOSITE An 18th-century engraving of the myth of Icarus.

THE BRUEGHEL VERSION

AROUND 1558 THE FLEMISH ARTIST PIETER BRUEGHEL
THE ELDER painted his *Landscape with the Fall of Icarus*
– although the painting we know today may be a copy by
another hand of a lost original. Brueghel's perspective
on the story is derived from Ovid, who writes: 'Some
angler catching fish with a quivering rod, or a shepherd
leaning on his crook, or a ploughman resting on the
handles of his plough, saw them, perhaps, and stood
there amazed, believing them to be gods able to travel
the sky.'

Brueghel's picture is dominated by a man
ploughing a field, while beyond him a shepherd tends his
flock and a great ship sails across the sea towards a
distant port, safety, and the setting sun. In the bottom
right-hand corner, easily overlooked, is a curious detail: it
is the leg of Icarus, the last part of him to disappear
under the waves after his fall. The incidental role
accorded the great myth in this painting has inspired two
famous poems. In W.H. Auden's 'Musée des Beaux Arts'
(1940), Icarus' splashdown from the ploughman's point of
view 'was not an important failure', while in William
Carlos Williams's 1962 sequence, *Pictures from Brueghel*,
the splash of Icarus drowning goes 'quite unnoticed'.

Thus the world shrugs at the vanity of ambition,
the folly of endeavour, and gets on with its work.

RIGHT *Landscape with the Fall of Icarus* by Pieter Bruegel the Elder.

'In tedious exile now too long
    detain'd,
Daedalus languish'd for his
    native land:
The sea foreclos'd his flight;
    yet thus he said:
Tho' Earth and water in
    subjection laid,
O cruel Minos, thy
    dominion be,
We'll go thro' air; for sure
    the air is free.'

Ovid, *Metamorphoses*, Book 8,
translated by Sir Samuel Garth, John Dryden, et al.

mother Europa by Zeus in the guise of a beautiful white bull. Many years later, another beautiful white bull appeared on Crete, sent by the sea god Poseidon, who told Minos to sacrifice the animal in his honour. But Minos kept the bull for himself and slaughtered another beast in its stead. In his anger, Poseidon made Pasiphaë, Minos' wife, lust after the bull from the sea, and to consummate her passion she secretly asked Daedalus to make a hollow wooden cow covered in hide, in which she hid herself and was mated by the bull. Thus, in Ovid's words, from her

monster-teeming womb, the Earth
Receiv'd, what much it mourn'd, a
bi-form birth.

This was the Minotaur, a monstrous man with the head of a bull, the living manifestation of Pasiphaë's shame. It was to hide this stain on the house of Minos that the king commissioned Daedalus to build the Labyrinth, a maze of dark tunnels under the palace, a maze through which no man could find his way, a maze

Where rooms within themselves encircled lie,
With various windings, to deceive the eye.

The Minotaur gorged on human flesh, and to feed its appetite Minos demanded that every ninth year the Athenians send a tribute of seven youths and seven maidens, who were abandoned to their gory fate in the dark of the Labyrinth. Amongst the third group of Athenians was Theseus, a prince with whom Minos' daughter Ariadne fell in love. Theseus succeeded in killing the Minotaur, and found his way out of the Labyrinth by following the thread he'd attached to the entrance and unwound as he wandered in search of the monster. He then sailed off with Ariadne to the island of Naxos, where, 'quickly cloy'd, ungrateful, and unkind', he abandoned her and returned to Athens.

The fury of the king

It was Daedalus who had provided Ariadne with the idea and the thread that had saved Theseus, and in his anger at this betrayal Minos shut up the master artificer in his own Labyrinth. Imprisoned with Daedulus was his son Icarus, who had been born to him by a slave girl in the palace. Daedalus yearned for his homeland, but Minos ruled both land and sea, so escape seemed impossible – until Daedalus came up with a bold idea: though earth and water were the dominions of King Minos, the air belonged only to the birds. So they would become like birds.

Daedalus set about fashioning wings from wax and wood and feathers, and, after a trial flight, he gave instructions to young Icarus:

> My boy, take care
> To wing your course along the middle air;
> If low, the surges wet your flagging plumes;
> If high, the sun the melting wax consumes:
> Steer between both: nor to the northern skies,
> Nor south Orion turn your giddy eyes;
> But follow me: let me before you lay
> Rules for the flight, and mark the pathless way.

As the old man fixed the wings to the boy a tear rolled down his cheeks, such was his fear for his son on this untried venture. He kissed him and embraced him, not knowing it was for the last time. Then, like a parent bird, he coaxed him into the liquid air, and cheered him on.

Northward they flew, with Delos and Paros to their left, Samos on the right. But Icarus, grown wild and wanton in his new element, flew higher than his father, soaring emboldened nearer and nearer to the sun – whose heat began to soften then to melt the wax that bound his feathers to their frame. The wings collapsed and down he fell, the useless quills flurrying playfully in the air about him, until at last he plunged into the waters forever after known as the Icarian Sea. Later his body washed up on the island called Icaria. Watching this disaster, a partridge flapped its wings and uttered cries of joy, remembering an earlier fall.

Rather than making landfall in Athens, the distraught Daedalus ended his flight hundreds of miles to the west, in Sicily, where he took refuge at the court of Cocalus, king of Camicus. Minos, still intent on revenge, sailed from kingdom to kingdom in search of Daedalus. At each port he would demand that the local ruler thread a spiral seashell. No one could do such an impossible thing until Minos arrived at Camicus, where Cocalus returned the shell, perfectly threaded. Minos knew that only Daedalus could achieve such a feat, and he was right: the old artificer, remembering his trick with the Labyrinth, had tied one end of the thread to an ant, which had crawled through the shell. Minos demanded that Cocalus hand over Daedalus, but Cocalus was pleased with the projects Daedalus had under-taken for him, and besides his daughters had

> ❝They say
> That Daedalus, when he fled
> the realm of Minos,
> Dared to entrust himself to
> stroking wings
> And to the air of heaven –
> unheard-of path –
> On which he swam away to
> the cold North ...❞
>
> Virgil, *Aeneid*, Book VI, trans.
> Robert Fitzgerald

grown fond of the old man. So fond, in fact, that as Minos sat in his bath before enjoying a banquet with his host, the daughters of Cocalus came to him and killed him by pouring boiling water all over his body.

The secrets of the Labyrinth

The story of Daedalus, the Labyrinth and the Minotaur was supposed pure myth until the beginning of the 20th century, when the British archaeologist Sir Arthur Evans began to excavate on Crete and uncovered the ruins of Knossos – the vast palace mentioned by Homer in the 8th century BC as the place where Daedalus built a dancing floor for Princess Ariadne (*The Iliad*, Book XIX, line 590). The complex maze of rooms and passageways irresistibly reminded Evans of the Labyrinth that Daedalus built for the Minotaur, while on the walls there were pictures of young men and women leaping over bulls – evidence of some kind of bull cult on the island, which presumably gave rise to the story of Pasiphaë and her unnatural child. *The Iliad* may recall the time of the Mycenaeans, the civilization on mainland Greece that flourished in the latter half of the second millennium BC. The civilization that Evans uncovered on Crete was much older, first emerging around 2200 BC, and coming to an abrupt end around 1450 BC – perhaps devastated by earthquake or volcanic eruption or Mycenaean invasion. Evans named this lost civilization after King Minos, and ever since these people have been known as Minoans.

MARY AND THE
PAGE BOY

Mary Queen of Scots escapes from Lochleven Castle, 1568

In the broad strath between the Ochil Hills and the Lomonds of Fife, in the shadow of the black basalt escarpments of Benarty Hill, lies the dark expanse of Loch Leven. Just before dusk in the early days of winter, when the grass has withered ash-pale on the hills, the air grows loud as skein after skein of geese fly in from the far north. Filling the twilight with their clamour, many come to land among the tussocks of St Serf's Island, home to a religious settlement for a thousand years until the last monks abandoned it in 1560, as the Reformation cut a swathe through Scotland. On a June night seven years later, a small boat could be seen crossing to another of the loch's small islands. Slumped in the stern, speechless with exhaustion and despair, sat Mary Queen of Scots. Her subjects had deemed that Lochleven Castle was from henceforth to be her prison.

The water level in the loch was higher then than it is today, and the island hardly extended beyond the great 14th-century keep and its surrounding walls and garden. In his novel *The Abbot* (1820), which tells of Mary's imprisonment here, Sir Walter Scott writes of 'the water-girdled fortress, which ... consisted only of one large donjon-keep, surrounded with a court-yard, with two round flanking-towers at the angles, which contained within its circuit some other buildings of inferior importance. A few old trees, clustered together near the castle, gave some relief to the air of desolate seclusion ...' It was in this grim place that Mary was forced to abdicate the crown of Scotland, the crown she'd worn since she was less than one week old.

The curse of the Stuarts

Mary Queen of Scots descended from a line of Stuart kings seemingly doomed to ill fortune and violent, premature death. With a succession of long minorities, royal authority in Scotland was often tenuous, with power in the kingdom surging to and fro between warring nobles – turbulent men who behaved as brutally and selfishly as Mafia dons. Mary's great-great-great grandfather James I had been assassinated in a monastery privy; *his* son James II was blown up by one of his own cannon; his son James III was murdered by the supporters of his own son, who as James IV led 10,000 Scots to defeat and slaughter at Flodden Field. Only Mary's father, James V, died peacefully in his bed – supposedly of heartache after his army was defeated by the English, and hearing that his wife had given birth to a girl. 'It cam with ane lass

---

PREVIOUS PAGE A contemporary French portrait of Mary Queen of Scots.

and it will pass with ane lass,' he is reported to have predicted on his death bed, referring to the Stuart line.

Thus Scotland was bequeathed the legacy of another long minority, and – a thing unheard of – a female on the throne. Within a couple of years Henry VIII of England, furious that the Scots would not agree to marry the infant Mary to his son and heir, the future Edward VI, embarked on what became known as the 'Rough Wooing'. English armies devastated much of southeastern Scotland, in pursuit of Henry's instructions to 'Put all to fire and sword.' This only served to strengthen the Scots' 'Auld Alliance' with the French, and in 1548 Mary was sent off to France to marry the dauphin. In 1559 the dauphin succeeded to the French throne as Francis II, and for a brief period, until Francis's death the following year, Mary was queen of two kingdoms – and claimant to a third throne, that of England, on the grounds that she was, like Elizabeth I, a descendant of Henry VII.

> *En ma fin gît mon commencement.*
>
> In my end is my beginning.

The motto of Mary Queen of Scots, embroidered on her clothing

A turbulent reign

After Francis's death, Mary returned to Scotland, which was then in the throes of the Protestant Reformation. Mary herself was a Catholic, but had the political sense not to oppose the reformers, and, indeed, authorized the suppression of the pro-Catholic rebellion of the Earl of Huntly, the so-called 'Cock of the North'. More contentious was the matter of her remarriage; she had not yet borne a child, and Scotland needed an heir. Elizabeth of England, her older, more powerful cousin, insisted on having a hand in the selection of Mary's second husband, and put forward her own favourite, the Earl of Leicester. To counter English influence, Mary's secretary, Maitland of Lethington, proposed a Spanish match, but the prince in question, Don Carlos, turned out to be insane. At this juncture, having fallen for her younger cousin Henry Stuart, Lord Darnley, Mary threw political good sense to the winds. Her marriage in 1565 to Darnley, a mean-spirited, violent, hard-drinking wastrel – and a Catholic to boot – alienated some of Mary's supporters, notably her bastard half-brother, the Earl of Moray, who had been her loyal counsellor but now rose in rebellion.

> *Et en rien n'ai plaisir Qu'en regret et désir.*
>
> Nothing now my heart can fire But regret and desire.

Lines from Mary's ode on the death of her first husband, Francis II

Moray's threat was short-lived, however, as Mary, accompanied by Darnley, pursued the rebels round Scotland in what was known as the Chaseabout Raid, and Moray was forced to take refuge in England.

Mary soon became pregnant with the future James VI, but her relations with her husband rapidly deteriorated. Darnley was petulant and jealous, especially of Mary's secretary, David Rizzio, and one night he and a group of followers butchered the little Italian in her presence at Holyroodhouse in Edinburgh. When Mary tried to

'No man pleaseth her that contenteth not him. And what may I say more, she hath given over unto him her whole will, to be ruled and guided as himself best liketh.'

Thomas Randolph, the English ambassador in Scotland, reports on Mary's marriage to Darnley in a letter to the Earl of Leicester, 31 July 1565. Mary was 22 when she married for the second time; Darnley was only 19.

call for help, one of the conspirators, Lindsay of the Byres, threatened to 'cut her in collops'. Within a year, in February 1567, the house in Edinburgh where Darnley was staying was blown up. He himself was found dead in the gardens, wearing only a nightshirt. It appeared that he had been strangled.

Darnley had acquired many enemies, but popular suspicions fell on one man in particular: the tough Border magnate, James Hepburn, Earl of Bothwell, who, it seems, was determined to marry the queen and to become master both of Mary and of Scotland. Suspicion also fell upon Mary herself, although no absolutely definitive proof of her involvement has ever been produced. Mary had already, the previous year, shown her devotion to the powerful Bothwell – so different to the callow youths she had hitherto married – by making a fifty-mile round trip on horseback in a single day to see him at his remote castle in Liddesdale, after hearing he had been wounded in an affray. It is possible that her motives were not in fact romantic, and that she was making a planned visit to him on matters of state. But in either case the incident demonstrates her reliance upon the great Border lord.

In April 1567 Bothwell was brought to trial in Edinburgh for his alleged part in the Darnley murder. He arrived with a troop of armed, mounted Hepburns in his train, and, according to one contemporary source, was 'made clean of the said slaughter, albeit that it was heavily murmured that he was guilty thereof'. Within two weeks of his acquittal, Bothwell encountered Mary as she travelled from Linlithgow Palace to Edinburgh. He rode at the head of 800 horsemen, and told Mary her life was in danger if she entered Edinburgh, and that she must accompany him to his castle at Dunbar. Here, it seems almost certain, he raped her – Mary herself hinting at this when she later wrote: 'Albeit we found his doings rude, yet were his answer and words but gentle.' Having consummated their relationship, it only remained for him to marry the queen, which he did on 15 May.

Wearied and almost broken

Some said the abduction and the alleged rape was just for show, that Mary was besotted with the man who had killed her previous husband. Mary, opined Sir William Kirkcaldy, 'shall go with him to the world's end in a white petticoat before she leaves him'. But others have since claimed it would be unlikely that Mary would fall into the trap of marrying out of infatuation a second time. She was, she wrote to Archbishop James Beaton just after her marriage to Bothwell, 'wearied and almost broken with the frequent uproars and rebellions raised against us since we came in Scotland'. It is thus more likely that she identified in Bothwell a man who could help her rule her unruly people, 'a people as factious amongst themselves and as factious toward the ruler as any other nation in Europe,' as she wrote to her cousin, Elizabeth of England. It was thus that she sought to justify the fact that she had married so precipitately, and without Elizabeth's approval – something she was anxious to obtain, as she wished her cousin to name her as heir to the English throne.

More problematic than the opinion of Elizabeth was the opinion of the fractious Scottish nobility: unsurprisingly, given the nature of Scottish politics, many of the great magnates were envious of Bothwell's sudden elevation (he was now Duke of Orkney), and determined to bring him down when it became clear that he had no intention of involving them in the rule of the land. They masked their true motives in moral indignation that the queen should have taken as her third husband the man widely believed to have been responsible for the death of her second. By the beginning of June Bothwell's enemies – led by Maitland, Mary's former ally, and the Earl of Morton – were in open rebellion. On 6 June Bothwell and Mary left Holyroodhouse for Borthwick Castle, to the south of Edinburgh. When the castle was surrounded, first Bothwell and then Mary, disguised as a man, managed to slip away. They proceeded by a roundabout route towards Edinburgh, but failed to gather the support they hoped for. On 15 June the small royal army was met at Carberry Hill, near Musselburgh, by a much larger rebel force. The insurgents, known as the Confederate Lords, rode under a banner depicting the corpse of Darnley,

> 'The Queen could not but marry him, seeing he had ravished her and laid with her against her will.'
>
> Sir James Melville, who had been in Dunbar Castle at the time of the abduction of Mary by the Earl of Bothwell

beside which knelt his infant son James. It bore the legend 'Judge and avenge my cause, O Lord.' (This, of course, was rank hypocrisy: Maitland, Morton and others among the rebels had joined with Bothwell in plotting against Darnley's life.) The Confederate Lords told Mary that if she gave up Bothwell she would be restored to her former power. She angrily refused. While Bothwell issued challenges to the rebel lords to engage in single combat with him, his own troops began to fade away. Eventually, seeing a pitched battle would be hopeless for the royalists, Bothwell suggested to Mary that they retreat to his great fortress at Dunbar. Mary, however, perhaps believing in the underlying loyalty of the rebels, and anxious to maintain the peace, agreed to go with them to Edinburgh, while obtaining a safe-conduct for her husband, who embraced her for the last time and rode hell for leather for Dunbar and eventual exile. She was never to see him again.

This woeful queen

Mary's humiliation now began. During her desperate wanderings, she had none of her own fine wardrobe with her, but was dressed in the borrowed clothes of a common townswoman. Where she expected cheers from the soldiers who escorted her, she received only taunts and insults. 'Burn the whore,' some shouted. 'Kill her, drown her!' others yelled. The Confederate Lords had done their job: her reputation among her subjects was thoroughly blackened. By the time she arrived in Edinburgh, Mary was distraught. Her humiliation continued when guards were posted inside the room she was kept in at the lord provost's house at Craigmillar. She cried out to her subjects through the window, and her captors, fearing that she might elicit the sympathy of the Edinburgh mob, resolved to remove her to a remote, secure prison.

Such was their haste that the queen was not even allowed to finish her supper – the first meal she had eaten since before the contretemps on Carberry Hill. So began the long ride through the gathering gloom to Loch Leven, via a boat across the Forth from Leith. Hearing of a possible rescue attempt, Mary had tried to keep a slow pace, but her guards, including Lord Ruthven and Lindsay of the Byres – the man who had threatened to cut her into collops after the murder of Rizzio – whipped on her horse. At last they came to the shore of the loch, from where she was accompanied across the water to the island fortress by its laird, Sir William Douglas, half-brother to the Earl of Moray and cousin to Morton. She had nothing with her but the clothes she wore, and the room she was lodged in had none of the comforts to which a queen was accustomed. Meanwhile the Confederate Lords in power in Edinburgh looted her possessions and took what they wanted for themselves. Exhausted and sick with despair and the early stages of pregnancy, Mary did not speak or eat for a fortnight.

Over time Mary gradually recovered her health and something of her former spirits. She firmly rebuffed all demands that she divorce Bothwell, probably because such an action would bastardize the child she now knew she was carrying. However, in July she had a miscarriage, and realized she had been bearing twins. Shortly after this tragedy, on 24 July, Lindsay of the Byres told the queen she must sign letters of abdication in favour of her one-year-old son, James, from whom she had been separated. Her half-brother, the Earl of Moray, was to become regent. If she refused, Lindsay said, he would cut her throat. James was duly crowned on 29 July, and the cannon in Lochleven Castle were fired in celebration. Mary wept.

But the rudely deposed queen was not without her sympathizers and admirers. Even the rough Lord Ruthven had gone down on his knees and promised to help her escape if she would return his love. She did not. In England, Queen

> **The event is indeed strange and otherwise nor (we know) you would have looked for. But as it has succeeded, we must take the best of it.**
>
> Mary Queen of Scots, on her marriage to Bothwell, in a letter to Archbishop James Beaton, 1567

> **Ah, Kingdom of Scotland, I think that your days are now shorter than they were, and your nights longer, since you have lost that princess who was your light.**
>
> Pierre de Bourdeille, Seigneur de Brantôme (c.1540–1614), *Memoirs*

Elizabeth was desperate for her cousin's safety, not least because if the Scots killed their anointed queen it would set an unfortunate precedent to her own people. So one of her ablest diplomats, Sir Nicholas Throckmorton, was sent north to dissuade the Scots from doing anything rash. Throckmorton himself was convinced that it was only his presence in Scotland that saved the life of the woman he referred as 'this woeful queen'.

Across the dark waters

For her part, Mary – who by now had acquired a small domestic staff and some of her former luxuries – began to plot how she might escape and recover the crown. A plan hatched by John Sempill, the son of Lord Sempill, to assault the castle at night came to nothing, but Mary – aware of the effect she could have on impressionable young men – turned her charms on the keeper's younger brother George Douglas – 'Pretty Geordie' – whom she used to convey messages to the outside world.

Winter came and with it the geese from the north. Showers of sleet scurried across the face of the Lomond Hills, cat's-paws fretting the grey waters of the loch. The days grew short, and the branches of the few trees round the castle stood black and bare. Then, in March 1568, with the land still in the grip of winter, Mary made her first escape attempt. She walked out disguised as a washerwoman, but the boatman rowing her to the mainland, annoyed that she covered her face, reached forward to remove her muffler. When she raised a hand to stop him, he noticed that her elegant fingers were 'fair and white', and realized this was no washerwoman. He rowed the queen back to the castle, but did not mention the incident to Sir William.

George Douglas – who had been expelled from the island following a row with his brother, the laird, and who seems to have conceived a notion of marrying Mary – worked hard on the queen's behalf. He first came up with an idea of smuggling Mary out in a box, but this was vetoed by the boatmen he bribed to take messages to and fro. Mary and George now involved a third figure in the Douglas household in their plans. 'Little Willie' Douglas – whom Mary dubbed 'Orphan Willie' – was a page in the castle and a cousin (or possibly an illegitimate child) of Sir William. Barely 16, he too came under the thrall of Mary's charms. However, the difficulties of escape were intensified after Sir Archibald Napier, Laird of Merchiston and father of the mathematician, made a curious prediction – as recounted by Mary's secretary, Claude Nau:

'It is by force alone that I can be delivered. If you send never so few troops to countenance the matter, I am certain great numbers of my subjects will rise to join them; but without that they are overawed by the power of the rebels and dare attempt nothing themselves.

Mary writes to the French queen, Catherine de Médicis, from Lochleven Castle, 1 May 1568

> The Laird of Markyston, who had the reputation of being a great wizard, made bets with several persons to the amount of five hundred crowns, that by the fifth of May Her Majesty would be out of Lochleven.

As a consequence of this curious circumstance, the guard on the queen was strengthened. Nevertheless, Mary was allowed to join in boating expeditions, during one of which her servants playfully reported she had escaped. The confusion that followed provided a useful distraction from the real escape plan.

The date set was 2 May. George Douglas, along with Lord Seton (Mary Seton's father) and Sir William Douglas's best horses, which had been 'borrowed' for the occasion, waited on the mainland, while Little Willie managed things in the castle. Initially he had suggested that Mary drop from the seven-foot perimeter wall, but when one of her ladies tried this and badly sprained her foot, this idea was abandoned. Willie realized he had to find a way of getting Mary out of the main gate. Given that it was the Mayday weekend, he proposed he lead the festivities as the Abbot of Unreason, and spent the day performing what everybody thought was a series of drunken japes – useful cover for unusual behaviour on his part, which included holing all the boats drawn up on the shore – all the boats except one. Sir William was suspicious, and kept an eye on the horsemen seen on the far shore, but failed to put two and two together. Mary added to the general confusion by pretending to faint, obliging Sir William to fetch her a glass of wine.

At supper time Mary withdrew to her own rooms, where she changed clothes with one of her ladies-in-waiting, Mary Seton, who was to stay behind to impersonate the queen. Meanwhile, as he served Sir William at table, Little Willie somehow managed to lay hold of the castle keys. He then went out into the courtyard, signalled to Mary to descend, and the two of them walked together through the main gate. Having locked the gate behind him, Willie threw the keys into the mouth of a cannon.

Once ashore, Mary and Willie were greeted by George Douglas and Lord Seton, and by midnight Mary had crossed the Firth of Forth and come safely to the Setons' seat at Niddry Castle, to the west of Edinburgh. After ten and a half months of confinement, Mary was once more at liberty – and once more, in her own eyes and in those of at least some of her people, queen of Scotland.

Her triumph was short-lived, however. In less than a fortnight, on 13 May 1568, the small army she had raised was defeated by the Confederate Lords at Langside, near Glasgow, where, according to one contemporary, 'there was father against son, and brother against brother'. Mary now, according to another contemporary, 'lost courage, which she did never before, and took so great fear that she rested never until she was in England'. Such was her panic, Mary later recalled, that she neither ate nor drank for 24 hours. In fleeing to England, she hoped to gain the support of Elizabeth, but politics intervened as the latter's caution overrode her feelings of kinship – and thus Mary found herself not a supplicant but a prisoner of her cousin.

ABOVE The execution of Mary Queen of Scots in the Great Hall at Fotheringhay, 8 February 1587.

During the course of the next two decades, hostility between Protestants and Catholics throughout Europe became more and more extreme. The pope excommunicated the Protestant Elizabeth, thus making it the duty of all Catholics to remove her from the throne of England and replace her with her Catholic cousin. Mary became involved in some of these plots, and in the end Elizabeth agreed, reluctantly, that Mary had to die. The end came on 7 February 1587, at Fotheringhay Castle. A contemporary left an account of her execution:

> Then ... one of the executioners holding of her slightly with one of his hands, she endured two strokes of the other executioner with an axe, she making very little noise or none at all, and not stirring any part of her from the place where she lay ... Then one of the executioners, pulling off her garters, espied her little dog which was crept under her clothes, which could not be gotten forth but by force, yet afterward would not depart from the dead corpse but came and lay between her head and her shoulders.

It was not only Mary's little dog that kept faith with her. Through all her captivity, right up to the end at Fotheringhay, Mary was attended by Little Willie Douglas, the page boy who had so ingeniously rescued her from Lochleven. He was rewarded by a mention in her will.

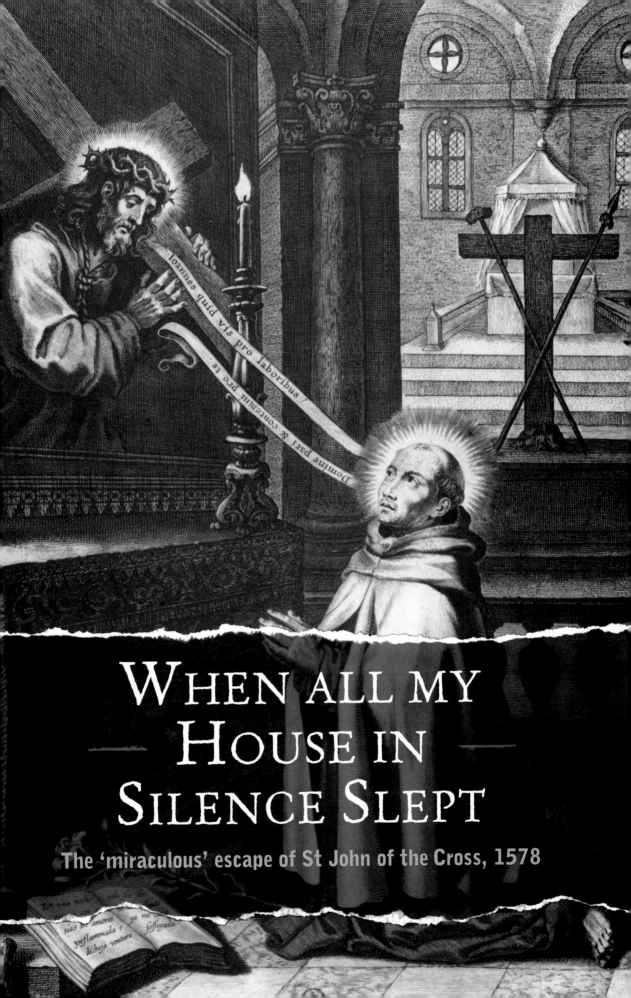

Ioannes quid vis pro laboribus?

Domine pati & contemni pro te

WHEN ALL MY HOUSE IN SILENCE SLEPT

The 'miraculous' escape of St John of the Cross, 1578

Along with his contemporary, St Teresa of Avila, St John of the Cross is regarded as one of the greatest of Christian mystics, who in his poetry expresses the experience of the union of the soul with Christ. He was also a noted theologian and reformer, and it was because of his efforts to simplify the monastic life of the Carmelites that he ended up a prisoner in Toledo. His escape, on 16 August 1578, has been attributed by the pious to divine intervention. Whether or not he was the recipient of supernatural aid, it was certainly a remarkable episode in an extraordinary life.

John – born Juan de Yepes Álvarez – had joined the Carmelite Order in 1563, aged just 21, and was ordained as a priest four years later. Subsequently Teresa of Avila asked him to help her in her efforts to reform the Order, and he joined her in establishing a number of new houses across Spain. They called themselves 'Discalced [i.e. barefoot] Carmelites', and followed a strict and austere rule, which met with considerable resistance from many others in the Order – the 'Calced' friars. On the night of 3 December 1577, after he had failed to obey a command from his superiors, John was seized by Calced friars and taken to the ancient Carmelite monastery in Toledo.

The dark night of the soul

This was the era of the Counter-Reformation, a dangerous time for any who fell foul of the ecclesiastical authorities. The Catholic Church in Spain was not only riven by jealousies and petty power struggles, it was also in a fervour of theological turmoil, and while the Church tried to reform itself from within, it was at the same time sensitive to any unauthorized deviation from strict orthodoxy. Between 1575 and 1610, in Toledo alone the Inquisition imposed 366 death sentences, resulting in public auto-da-fés in which the victims were tied to stakes and burnt alive.

The established Carmelite Order considered John guilty not only of disobedience but also of rebellion, and he was thus deemed excommunicate. He was punished accordingly, forbidden the Mass and the sacraments, and confined in a stifling cell so

'Where have you hidden,
Beloved, and left me
    moaning?
You fled like the stag after
    wounding me;
I went out calling you,
    but you were gone.'

St John of the Cross, *Spiritual Canticle*, stanza 1, in which the Bride (the soul) addresses the Bridegroom (Christ); translated by Kieran Kavanaugh and Otilio Rodriguez.

PREVIOUS PAGE An 18th-century engraving of St John of the Cross, representing the mystical union with Christ celebrated by John in his poems.

small that there was barely room even for a man of his slight build, with the only light and air coming from a small slit high in one corner. Throughout his imprisonment John was subjected to regular public 'discipline', being forced to kneel half naked as the friars took it in turns to whip his bared back, while one of their number charged him to renounce the reformed rule he had helped to establish. His persecutors were further incensed when he met their frenzied attacks with only stillness and silence, and such was the ferocity of the lashings that his woollen tunic became crusted with blood. He was to bear the scars for the rest of his life.

> 'In safety, in disguise,
> In darkness up the secret
>   stair I crept,
> (O happy enterprise)
> Concealed from other eyes
> When all my house at
>   length in silence slept.'
>
> St John of the Cross, 'Songs of the Soul in Rapture', translated by Roy Campbell

With his outer silence came inner peace. It was while he was imprisoned that John composed many of the poems for which he is most famous, including parts of the *Spiritual Canticle* and *The Dark Night of the Soul*. In these verses, some of the finest in Spanish literature, John achieves an intimate communion with his God, as the soul and Christ become lover and beloved:

> Oh night that was my guide!
> Oh darkness dearer than the morning's pride,
> Oh night that joined the lover
> To the beloved bride
> Transfiguring them each into the other.
>
> (translation by Roy Campbell)

He was aided in his composition by the arrival of a more sympathetic warder, and this friar passed him paper, enabling him to record the progress of his spiritual quest. But as John's soul reached out to his God, his body wasted away with ill treatment and malnutrition. So weak was he that when one day the prior in charge of the monastery paid him a visit he did not stir. The prior, irritated, jabbed his foot into John's side, demanding to know why he did not stand in his presence. John begged his pardon; he had not recognized him, and his wounds prevented him from rising. The prior asked what had so distracted his mind. John replied that he had been thinking that the morrow was the Feast of the Virgin Mary, and how he wished he could once more say Mass. 'Not in my time,' the prior retorted, as he turned on his heel and left.

A leap in the dark

According to the saint's hagiographers, the following day, 15 August 1578, the Virgin Mary appeared to John, prompting him to escape, and advising him how he might achieve this. In his mind's eye, so they say, he saw a window in the corridor beyond his cell, high above the River Tagus. This window was where he was to make his

'I regard his flight as miraculous, and ordained by Our Lord, in order that he might help the reform of the Discalced. And, although I was deprived of my rights and privileges for some days, still, in spite of all, I was glad that he had escaped, and so were some other brothers, because we had compassion for him, seeing him suffer with so much courage.'

Deposition of Friar Juan de Santa-Maria, St John's sympathetic warder, quoted in Fr. Bruno of Jesus and Mary, *St Jean de la Croix* (1929)

exit, after loosening the screws in the padlock of his cell. This last procedure he managed bit by bit, a few turns at a time. While the other friars were dining in the refectory, his warder allowed him to leave his cell to empty his bucket and collect water for washing – the procedure now known by prisoners as 'slopping out'. He took this opportunity to reconnoitre the window, and, with the aid of a thread tied to a stone, he measured the distance to the ground. He had made himself a rope, improvised out of blankets and a strip of his tunic, but now he realized it was not long enough to reach the ground. He would need to trust in God and jump.

On the night of 16 August he consummated his plan. As he opened the first door he saw two visiting friars asleep in the next-door room. John was startled, the loosened padlock clattered to the floor, and one of the sleeping figures stirred and asked 'Who's there?' – but receiving no answer turned over and went back to sleep. The door beyond was open, to let the night air of August cool the oven-like interior of the monastery, and so John made his way without hindrance past the slumbering figures to the corridor window, where he attached his rope to a joist and began to lower himself into the dark abyss beneath. Swinging in space at the end of his rope he made his leap of faith, falling some ten feet onto a grass embankment. Had he misjudged his jump by only a foot or so, he would have fallen much further, down onto the rocks on the bank of the river far below. Picking himself up he did not know which way to go, but, coming across a dog feeding on discarded scraps he gave chase and followed it as it jumped down into a lower courtyard. Now he found himself faced with a high wall, and, despairing that he would ever be able to climb it, he slumped at its foot. All the while he had believed himself guided by the Virgin Mary and now, he later recalled, he felt himself lifted over this obstacle and deposited on the other side, in an alley of the city. He was at liberty once more. It certainly was a remarkable escape for a man in his poor physical condition.

In the small hours of the morning John made his way through the streets of Toledo to St Joseph of Carmel, a convent of Discalced nuns, who sheltered him for a while before sending him on to the Hospital of Santa Cruz, close to the monastery from which he had escaped. Here, ironically, he remained safe, while the Calced friars subjected the convent of St Joseph to a thorough search.

John gradually recovered his strength, and in due course the rift that had caused his imprisonment was healed. John went on to found more monasteries for the Discalced Carmelites, and he himself became vicar provincial for Andalusia. But when, towards the end of his life, the Order he had helped to found fell prey to dissension and schism, John withdrew into a silence and solitude that was absolute. He died on 14 December 1591. John was declared a saint by Pope Benedict XIII in 1726, and honoured as a Doctor of the Church in 1926, exactly two centuries after his canonization.

FATHER GERARD ESCAPES FROM THE TOWER

IN ENGLAND DURING THE REIGN OF QUEEN ELIZABETH I all Catholics came under suspicion as dangerous subversives – none more so than the Jesuit priests who trained on the Continent and were then infiltrated back into England. Notable among these priests was Father John Gerard. Despite disguising himself as a 'gentleman of moderate means', he was eventually caught in 1594 and imprisoned. Three years later, in April 1597, he was transferred to the Tower of London. Here he was subjected to torture, being suspended by his wrists, but never gave away the names of his associates. During his confinement he sent out coded messages to his Catholic supporters on the outside, and on 5 October 1597, despite his weakened condition and his damaged hands, he and a fellow prisoner made their way to a high wall overlooking the Tower Ditch. Here a waiting boatman threw up a rope, which they attached to a cannon, while the other end was secured on the other side of the ditch. They then swung down the rope, and were once more at liberty. Gerard remained underground in England and subsequently became close to the Gunpowder Plotters, although he remained ignorant of their plans. After the plot was foiled in November 1605 he was a wanted man, and fled to the Continent in the entourage of the ambassadors of Flanders and Spain. He died in Rome in 1637.

THE ROYAL OAK

Charles II hides up a tree, 1651

After 'The Red Lion' and 'The Crown', 'The Royal Oak' is the most common pub name in Britain. More than five hundred establishments bear the name, and the signs outside these pubs nearly all feature an oak tree, sometimes with a crown in its branches, sometimes with a portrait of King Charles II. A few depict a ship of the line, for in the history of the Royal Navy there have been eight warships named HMS *Royal Oak*, the last of which was the battleship sunk by a German U-boat in Scapa Flow at the beginning of the Second World War.

All these pubs and ships commemorate the extraordinary escape of Charles II after his final defeat by Oliver Cromwell, at the Battle of Worcester in 1651. While Commonwealth troops hunted high and low for the fugitive king, Charles hid in a great oak tree in the grounds of Boscabel House in Shropshire. Thus the king evaded captivity, and eventually made his way to exile on the Continent – from where, nine years later, he was to return in triumph to reclaim his kingdom.

Defeat at Worcester

According to Royalists, Charles had succeeded to the throne upon the execution of his father, Charles I, in January 1649. According to Parliament, however, England was now a republic. Charles II, in impoverished exile in the Netherlands, sought allies and cash wherever he could; he was not, unlike his father, one to stand on principle, for he had none. First, in 1650, he called on his loyal Scottish supporter, the Marquis of Montrose, to raise the Highland clans against the Covenanters then in power in Scotland. But when Montrose was defeated and captured, Charles promptly switched allegiances. He accepted the Covenant, so allowing the Scots to run their own Presbyterian Church without royally appointed bishops, and in return they crowned him king of Scotland on 1 January 1651. Then, at the head of a Scottish army, he marched south to reclaim the throne of England.

This last throw of the dice for the Royalist cause came to grief at Worcester on 3 September 1651. Charles and the Scots had occupied the city and strengthened its defences, but they faced an opposing army twice their own size. The English citizenry, fearing that their lands were to be taken by the Scots, paid no heed to Charles's calls to rally to his standard. For their part, the Scottish soldiery were exhausted after three weeks of marching, and their clothes were in tatters. Many even lacked shoes.

'The enemy is in Worcester,' Cromwell calmly recorded, 'and within a few days will have to fight or fly.' According to *A True and Faithful Narrative of Oliver*

OPPOSITE A symbolic depiction dating from 1660 of the Royal Oak at Boscabel. The three crowns represent Charles II's three kingdoms of England, Scotland and Ireland.

Cromwell's Compact with the Devil, a piece of contemporary Royalist propaganda, the Parliamentary commander prepared for the battle by striking a bargain with Old Nick himself, by which the latter would grant the former victory and seven years' prosperity.

Charles himself was prominent in the initial Royalist attack, one of his officers declaring, 'Certainly a braver prince never lived, having in the day of the fight hazarded his person much more than any officer of his army, riding from regiment to regiment.' But it was to no avail against overwhelming odds. George Downing, a Commonwealth officer, left an account of the battle:

> The dispute was from hedge to hedge and very hot; sometimes more with foot than with horse and foot. The lifeguard made a gallant charge, and so did my lord general's regiment of horse … The dispute continued to the evening, all along with great heat; and about sunset, we had beaten them into Worcester …

The Royalists, according to one of their number, 'were so dispersed that they rallied no more, but gave back violently, and forced the king to make into the town'. The Earl of Clarendon, in his *History of the Rebellion*, recounts that 'such a general consternation possessed the whole army, that the rest of the horse fled and all the foot threw down their arms before they were charged'. The Commonwealth forces pressed their advantage, seized Fort Royal, guarding the southeastern gate of the city, and turned its guns on the Royalists scurrying pell-mell through the gate, 'much readier to cut each other's throats' than to make a stand.

'Certainly a braver prince never lived.'

Unnamed Royalist officer, describing Charles's conduct at the Battle of Worcester

Charles tried to rally his forces, but in vain. 'I had rather you would shoot me,' he shouted at his fleeing men, 'rather than let me live to see the consequences of this day!' According to Clarendon, 'All was confusion; there were few to command, and none to obey.' The king retreated to his quarters in Cornmarket, and just as Commonwealth dragoons entered the front door, he slipped out the back and mingled with the fleeing crowds, and so made his escape from the city. Cromwell thanked God (or the Devil) for 'a very glorious mercy'. It was, he said, 'a total defeat and ruin of the enemy's army'. And so it was. The Battle of Worcester was the last fight of the English Civil Wars: 2,000 Royalists lay dead on the field; 10,000 were taken prisoner.

A king aloft

Charles left Worcester by St Martin's Gate, and took the road north. It was the beginning of a great adventure that was to test his mettle to the uttermost – and to provide him with a story to tell again and again through his reign, until his courtiers became bored of hearing it. As he and a few attendant lords pressed northward, they struggled to find their way through the darkness. Among those with the king was

Charles Giffard, the Catholic owner of the out-of-the-way Boscabel estate, some miles north of Worcester. It was suggested that the king take refuge in this remote place.

At dawn they arrived at Whiteladies, a safe house on the estate, and Charles changed his clothes for those of a woodman – green jerkin, grey breeches, leather doublet and greasy hat.

Initially, Charles planned to head incognito and alone to the republican heartland of London, the last place his enemies would think of looking for him. He and his party feared Commonwealth search parties, and once the sun was up Charles, accompanied only by Richard Penderel, a local yeoman farmer, took refuge in a nearby coppice, where the king spent the day without food or drink as troops passed by on the nearby road. It was during the course of this uncomfortable day that Charles was persuaded to head for the Welsh ports, as Penderel could think of no loyal family with whom the king could stay between Boscabel and London.

Once darkness returned, Charles and Penderel left the wood, and headed for the Severn, the great river that barred the way into Wales. But when they eventually reached it, they found all the bridges and all the boats guarded. They had no choice but to return to Boscabel, arriving at five o'clock in the morning of Saturday 6 September. Here Charles heard that Major Carlis or Careless, who had fought to the end for his king at Worcester, was hiding in the dense Boscabel Wood.

It was, according to Charles's account, himself who selected the large and noble oak in whose arms he and the major would spend the day. There was a little clearing round about it,

helping them to see if any troops approached. Indeed they did. 'We see the soldiers going up and down, in the thicket of the wood,' the king later told the diarist Samuel Pepys, 'searching for persons escaped, we seeing them now and then peeping out of the wood.' In between such alarms and excursions the exhausted king nodded off, his head resting on a cushion nestling on Carlis's lap. The major thereafter changed his name to Carlos, the Spanish version of Charles, in commemoration of his intimate association with the king.

Six weeks of wandering

When Charles returned to dine at Boscabel House that night, he learnt that there was a reward of £1000 for the capture of 'Charles Stuart, son of the late Tyrant'. Though, over the next days and weeks, scores of Royalist sympathizers knew of his whereabouts, none of them was to give him away. Charles spent that night in a

Some other royal escapes

THE WHITE CLOAK. During the middle of the 12th century, England was troubled by 'the Anarchy', a period of intermittent warfare between Stephen and Matilda, two rival claimants to the throne. In the summer of 1141 Matilda's army was routed as it attempted to lay siege to Winchester, and she was forced to flee. A story arose that she escaped to her stronghold at Devizes in Wiltshire by disguising herself as a corpse being taken for burial. The more prosaic truth was that she fled in such haste – riding her horse astride like a man – that she became exhausted, and had to be carried on a litter between two horses. At the end of the following year, Matilda found herself once more in peril, as Stephen's army besieged her in Oxford. One night she and a small escort of three or four knights slipped out of a side gate and made their way across the frozen Thames and the snow-covered fields to Abingdon, wearing white cloaks as camouflage. Eventually she reached safety at Devizes, but gradually her support in England drained away, and in 1148 she abandoned the struggle and returned to Normandy.

HUNTINGTOWER. In August 1582 the 16-year-old James VI of Scotland (later, as James I, the first Stuart king of England), was seized in the so-called 'Ruthven Raid' by William Ruthven, 1st Earl of Gowrie. Gowrie, the head of Scotland's more militant Protestants, objected to the influence on the boy-king of his favourite, Esmé Stuart, Duke of Lennox, who was suspected of Catholic sympathies. Gowrie held James in Ruthven Castle, near Perth, for nearly a year in an attempt to reassert his influence over the terrified young king. But in June 1583 James succeeded in escaping, and the following year Gowrie mounted the scaffold. James's retribution went further: the very name of Ruthven was proscribed, and Ruthven Castle became known by its present name, Huntingtower.

THE WINTER QUEEN. Over the centuries various other members of the Stuart dynasty were involved in dramatic escapes from their enemies. Mary Queen of Scots, the mother of James VI and I, had made a daring escape from Lochleven Castle in 1568 (see pp. 15-24); James's grandson, Charles II, was forced into a number of disguises and up an oak tree after his defeat at Worcester (this chapter), and his great-great-grandson, Bonnie Prince Charlie, was to spend five months zigzagging around the Highlands and Islands of Scotland with a price of £30,000 on his head (see pp. 53-62). James's own daughter, Elizabeth, had her own adventures. In 1613 she married a fellow-Protestant, Frederick, the Elector Palatine, who in 1619 accepted the throne of Bohemia, and was crowned that November. However, his rule was unpopular, and a year later he was defeated by Catholic forces at White Mountain, and he and his heavily pregnant wife were forced to flee via Berlin to the Netherlands. As their enemies had predicted, the reign of Frederick and Elizabeth had not lasted much more than a single winter.

> My troubles make me forget myself; I thank you all.

Charles II says farewell to the Penderel brothers who helped him to escape

cramped priest hole at the top of Boscabel House, but knew he could not stay long. Setting off for Moseley Old Hall, another safe house, he complained that his horse was too slow. 'My liege,' Penderel's brother Humphrey replied, 'can you blame the horse to go heavily, when he has the weight of three kingdoms on his back?' Charles got away from Boscabel just in time: that Monday the house was searched.

Charles's peripatetic adventures around the West Midlands continued. He swapped his disguise as a woodman for that of a servant called William Jackson, although he proved incapable of doffing his hat with the expected servility. On one occasion a blacksmith gave him the 'good news' that Cromwell had defeated 'those rogues the Scots'. With typical audacity, 'Will Jackson' then asked whether 'that rogue Charles Stuart' had yet been captured and hanged as he deserved. 'Spoken like an honest man,' replied the blacksmith. It was a sobering reminder of the peril he was in, and of the opinion of many in England that had brought him to this pass.

'Will Jackson' was supposedly in the employ of Jane Lane, the resourceful daughter of a Royalist colonel, and with this lady and her small entourage the king made his way southwards, towards the great port of Bristol. But at Bristol they could find no ship to take the king safely to the Continent, and so the party pressed on to

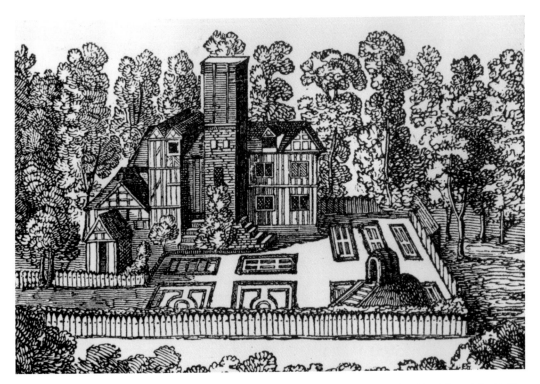

ABOVE A 17th-century engraving of Boscobel House, where Charles II took refuge after his defeat at the Battle of Worcester.

the West Country, where there were more Royalist sympathizers, and quiet little harbours where Charles might slip on board a boat and across the Channel.

Eventually it was arranged that on 22 September, for a fee of £60, a certain Captain Limbry would convey Charles to France from Charmouth, a Dorset fishing village near Lyme Regis. Limbry was told that he would be assisting the elopement of a young couple, a story intended to explain why the rendezvous was to be at eleven o'clock at night. But when the hour came, Limbry's vessel failed to appear; it turned out that his wife suspected that he was helping Royalists to escape, and locked him in his bedroom to keep him out of trouble.

Charles was obliged to renew his wanderings. He spent some time at Trent Manor, secluded in a deep valley near Sherborne, a hiding place one Royalist lady described as 'the Ark in which God shut him up when the floods of rebellion had covered the face of his dominions'. Eventually it was decided the West Country ports were too dangerous, packed as they were with crowds of Commonwealth troops preparing to embark for a campaign in the Channel Islands. Charles, now disguised as 'something like the meaner sort of gentleman', made his way eastward to Sussex, and the small port of Shoreham, whence on 15 October, at four in the morning, he set sail with a Captain Tattershall on board a collier called the *Surprise*.

Charles's six weeks of adventures after his defeat at Worcester were over. The voyage passed without incident, and the king was put ashore at Fécamp, near Rouen, to resume his long exile in France. When, nine years later, his exile eventually came to an end, Charles did not forget those who had helped him at peril of their own lives. Jane Lane was rewarded with a jewel worth a thousand pounds; the Penderel brothers received pensions and were presented at court; and the *Surprise* was purchased by the king and used by him as a yacht, renamed the *Royal Escape*.

After the Restoration, an Act of Parliament of 1664 specified that a special service of thanksgiving for the king's escape be included in the Book of Common Prayer (where it remained until 1859), and that the king's birthday, 29 May – which was also the day he re-entered London in 1660 – should be celebrated as Oak-Apple Day or Royal Oak Day. On that day for many years people wore sprigs of oak with gilded oak-apples in celebration of the Royal Oak of Boscabel.

THE BOSCABEL OAK TODAY

THE ROYAL OAK OF BOSCABEL became a victim of its own fame, for during the 17th and 18th centuries tourists in search of souvenirs cut off so much of the tree that it eventually died. The present 'Royal Oak' at Boscabel is in fact a descendant of the original. It was badly damaged in a storm in 2000, but the following year Prince Charles planted a sapling close by the old tree, grown from one of its acorns.

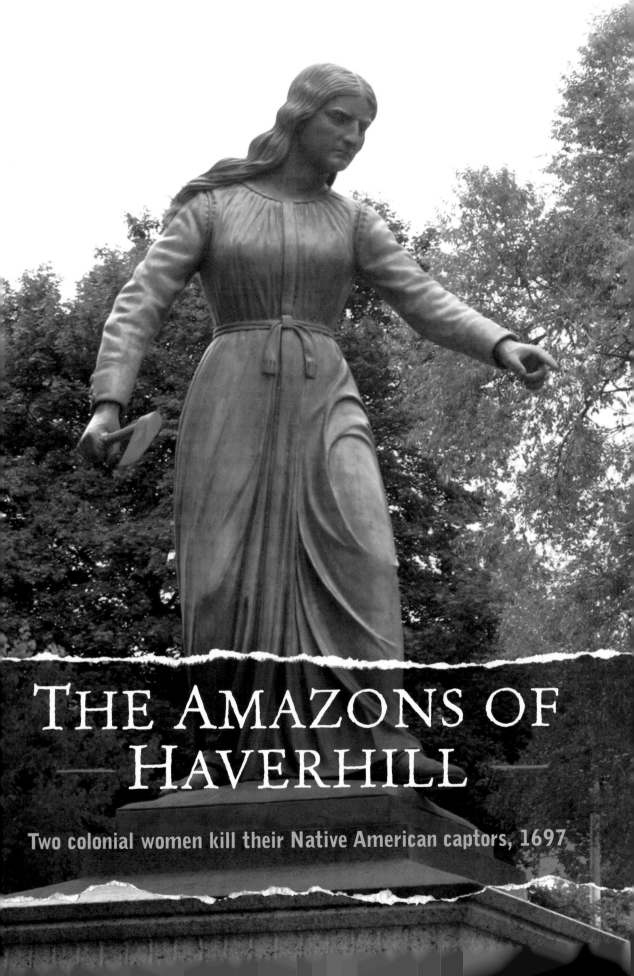

THE AMAZONS OF
— HAVERHILL —

Two colonial women kill their Native American captors, 1697

Today in Haverhill, Massachusetts, there stands a dramatic bronze statue of a woman wielding a tomahawk. The statue, thought to be the first to commemorate an American woman, was erected in 1879, and it depicts Hannah Dustin, who, captured by Native Americans, succeeded in killing ten of them while they slept, before making good her escape.

Her story comes down to us largely through *The Ecclesiastical History of New England* (1702) by the Reverend Cotton Mather, who obtained the details from Hannah herself. For Mather, Hannah's escape from her captors illustrated the workings of Divine Providence, and the certainty that God's favoured people were white English-speaking Protestant settlers. For more recent historians, Hannah's story illustrates the brutal clash that in the end was to see the virtual annihilation of Native American culture.

Hannah Emerson Dustin (1657–*c*.1736) was the daughter of Michael and Hannah Emerson, two of the early settlers of Haverhill. This was a time of religious zealotry in New England – the Salem Witch Trials took place in the early 1690s – and it seemed that half the population, convinced of its own righteousness, was equally convinced of the sinfulness of the other half. Thus, while Hannah Dustin, who killed six Native American children in the course of her escape, was to emerge as a colonial heroine, her younger sister Elizabeth was to be vilified as a whore and a murderess.

When she was just a girl, Elizabeth Emerson's father beat her so badly that he was taken to court. Some years later, in 1686, she was delivered of an illegitimate daughter. Five years after that, in 1691, she gave birth to illegitimate twins, who died shortly afterwards – whether of natural causes or by their mother's hand is unknown, but in either case she buried them secretly in her parents' garden. Concealing the death of a bastard child was still a capital offence in Massachusetts, and Elizabeth was convicted and sentenced to death. But for two years she was placed under the care of the Reverend Cotton Mather, who, though damning Elizabeth's 'haughty and stubborn spirit' and declaring 'there never was prisoner more hard-hearted', claimed that he succeeded in getting her to confess. She was hanged on 8 June 1693.

Bloody devastations

Elizabeth's sister Hannah, whose story begins four years after her sister's ended on the gallows, was to fare better. She had married Thomas Dustin (or Duston or Dustan) and borne him eight children the youngest of whom was only a few days old when a band of Abenaki, an Algonquian tribe, attacked the settlement. 'On

---

PREVIOUS PAGE The statue of Hannah Dustin in Haverhill, Massachusetts, complete with the tomahawk she used to slaughter her Native American captors.

March 15, 1697,' writes Mather, 'the salvages made a descent upon the skirts of Haverhill, murdering and captivating about thirty-nine persons, and burning about half a dozen houses.' As they approached the Dustin house 'with designs to carry on their bloody devastations', Thomas, despairing of being able to help his wife and baby daughter, fled with the seven older children 'until, by the singular providence of God, he arrived safe with them all unto a place of safety about a mile or two from his house'.

> '... their Indian master sometimes when he saw them dejected, would say unto them, "What need you trouble yourself? If your God will have you delivered, you shall be so!" And it seems our God would have it so to be.'
>
> The Reverend Cotton Mather, *Magnalia Christi Americana*; or *The Ecclesiastical History of New England* (1702)

Hannah had with her a nurse, Mary Neff, who tried to escape with the infant, but fell into the hands of the Abenaki. Hannah too was taken, and with a dozen or so other captives was led away by the 'furious tawnies'. The raiders 'dash'd out the brains of the infant against a tree', and, if any of the captives showed signs of exhaustion on the subsequent march, their captors 'would presently bury their hatchets in their brains and leave their carcases on the ground for birds and beasts to feed upon'.

Over the next few days, Hannah and Mary, now allocated to an Abenaki family of 'two stout men, three women, and seven children', travelled some 150 miles. The family were in fact Christians, although having been converted by the French, they were Catholic, and thus doubly loathsome to the Reverend Mather. At some point they were joined by another European captive, Samuel Lennardson, a youth of 14 who had been taken from Worcester, Massachusetts a year and a half previously. They were told that when they reached their destination, a town somewhere beyond what is now Penacook, New Hampshire:

> ... they must be stript, and scourg'd, and run the gauntlet through the whole army of Indians. They said this was the fashion when the captives first came to a town; and they derided some of the faint-hearted English, which, they said, fainted and swooned away under the torments of this discipline.

They bow'd, they fell, they lay down

Perhaps it was this prospect that inspired Hannah to take the course of action she now embarked upon. She was also, according to the Reverend Mather, fortified by the Old Testament story of Jael, wife of Heber, who hammered a tent peg into the head of Sisera the Canaanite. Having 'heartened the nurse and the youth to assist her in this enterprise', she waited until nightfall, and after their captors had fallen asleep they laid hold of their tomahawks. Then:

> ... they struck such home blows upon the heads of their sleeping oppressors, that ere they could any of them struggle into any effectual resistance, 'at the

feet of these poor prisoners, they bow'd, they fell, they lay down; at their feet they bow'd, they fell; where they bow'd, there they fell down dead'. Only one squaw escaped, sorely wounded, from them in the dark; and one boy, whom they reserved asleep, intending to bring him away with them, suddenly waked, and scuttled away from this desolation.

Before making good their escape in their captors' canoe down the Merrimack River, the two women and the boy cut off the scalps of those they had slaughtered: two men, two women and six children. Hannah later told a certain Samuel Sewall of Boston, who recorded it in his diary, that the night before the killings one of the Abenaki men had shown young Samuel Lennardson 'how he used to knock Englishmen on the head and take off their scalps; little thinking that the captives would make some of their first experiment upon himself'.

> ' ... being where she had not her own life secured by any law unto her, she thought she was not forbidden by any law to take away the life of the murderers by whom her child had been butchered. '
>
> The Reverend Cotton Mather, *Magnalia Christi Americana*; or *The Ecclesiastical History of New England* (1702)

When they reached Haverhill, Hannah was reunited with her husband and children; until this moment, she had not known whether they lived or had, like her baby, been put to death. She produced ten scalps as evidence of their actions, and on her behalf Thomas Dustin petitioned the General Court of Massachusetts for a reward for this 'just slaughter of so many of the Barbarians'. The scalpers duly received a bounty of 50 pounds – half to Hannah, the remainder divided between Mary and Samuel. Various gifts came to them from well-wishers in Boston, while the governor of Maryland, hearing of their deed, sent them 'a very generous token of his favour'. Hannah became the toast of the colonies.

Justifying Hannah

According to the Reverend Mather, Hannah defended her actions in slaughtering so many innocents thus: 'being where she had not her own life secured by any law unto her, she thought she was not forbidden by any law to take away the life of the murderers by whom her child had been butchered'. Later American writers retelling the story of Hannah, the heroic frontierswoman, also found it necessary to address the moral dimensions of her deed. Timothy Dwight, in his *Travels in New England and New York* (1821), approached the question thus:

> Whether all their sufferings, and all the danger of suffering anew, justified this slaughter may be questioned by you or some other exact moralist ... [But] a wife who had just seen her house burnt, her infant dashed against a tree, and her companions coldly murdered one by one; who supposed her husband and her remaining children, to have shared the same fate, who was threatened with

torture, and indecency more painful than torture ... would probably feel no necessity ... of asking questions concerning anything, but the success of the enterprise.

John Greenleaf Whittier, in *The Legends of New England* (1831), casts Hannah's story as one of revenge – the revenge of a mother half crazed with grief following the killing of her infant:

> The Savage held it before him for a moment, contemplating, with a smile of grim fierceness, the terrors of its mother, and then dashed it from him with all his powerful strength. Its head smote heavily on the trunk of an adjacent tree, and the dried leaves around were sprinkled with brains and blood. She has often said, that at this moment, all was darkness and horror – that her very heart seemed to cease beating, and to lie cold and dead in her bosom, and that her limbs moved only as involuntary machinery. But when she gazed around her and saw the unfeeling savages, grinning at her and mocking her, and pointing to the mangled body of her infant with fiendish exultation, a new and terrible feeling came over her. It was the thirst of revenge; and from that moment her purpose was fixed.

Whittier thus adds layers of melodramatic detail of his own imagining, while concealing the fact that six of her victims were mere children. Instead, he implies that they were all adult male warriors, except the little boy who escapes. Here Whittier quite outrageously twists the facts to suit the sentimental inclinations of his 19th-century audience:

> Mrs Dustin lifted her dripping hatchet above his head, but hesitated to strike the blow. 'It is a poor boy,' she said, mentally, 'a poor child, and perhaps he has a mother!' The thought of her own children rushed upon her mind and she spared him.

In sharp contrast, Nathaniel Hawthorne – obsessed with the dark stories of Puritan New England – turns the received moral universe upside down in his 1836 piece, 'The Duston Family'. He condemns Mather as 'an old hard-hearted, pedantic bigot' for damning the Catholic Abenaki. For Hawthorne, the latter are noble savages, softened by their Christianity, for ' ... what can be more touching than to think of these wild Indians, in their loneliness and their wanderings, wherever they went among the dark mysterious woods, still keeping up domestic worship'? He reserves his greatest vituperation for Hannah herself:

'Would that the bloody old hag ... had sunk over head and ears in a swamp, and been there buried, until summoned forth to confront her victims at the Day of Judgement ...'

Nathaniel Hawthorne condemns Hannah Dustin in 'The Duston Family' (1836)

Would that the bloody old hag had been drowned in crossing Contocook river, or that she had sunk over head and ears in a swamp, and been there buried, until summoned forth to confront her victims at the Day of Judgement; or that she had gone astray and been starved to death in the forest, and nothing ever seen of her again, save her skeleton, with the ten scalps twisted around it for a girdle.

A decade later, Henry David Thoreau retold Hannah's story in *A Week on the Concord and the Merrimack* (1849). He does not disguise the fact that women and children were among her victims; but for him it is a story of a distant, cruel past. He refers to the tradition that many claim to have 'eaten of the fruit of that apple tree' on which the baby's brains were dashed out. He concludes, conscious of the allusion to the Biblical story of the Forbidden Fruit and the Fall: 'This seems a long time ago, and yet it happened since Milton wrote his Paradise Lost ... From this September afternoon, and these now cultivated shores, those times seem more remote than the dark ages.' But perhaps those times were not so remote after all, for there still remained, after Thoreau wrote those words, half a century or more in which the white man would inflict appalling depredations upon the original inhabitants of the continent he claimed for his own.

His History will Astonish!

The multiple jail breaks of the
thief and folk hero Jack Sheppard, 1724

For all too short a span, young Jack Sheppard was the most glamorous figure of the London underworld. Within the space of a single year he escaped from jail, and thus the noose, no fewer than four times – on two occasions from the notorious Newgate Prison. But in the end his luck ran out, and following his fifth arrest, at the age of only 22, he was sent to the scaffold, while the ladies of London lined the streets and wept at his passing.

Sheppard's exploits inspired ballads even during his own lifetime, and plays such as *Harlequin Sheppard* and *The Prison-Breaker* swept the London stage soon after his death. The sensation surrounding his career prompted Jonathan Swift to suggest the idea of a 'Newgate pastoral' to John Gay, and the result was the spectacularly successful *Beggar's Opera*. Sheppard continued to achieve a kind of immortality – for example as William Hogarth's Idle Apprentice in his series of prints, *Industry and Idleness*, and, a century later, as the inspiration behind Charles Dickens's Artful Dodger, the impudent young pickpocket in *Oliver Twist*. Dickens, however, was at pains to point out that he had no intention of glamorizing crime, and sought to distance himself from the sensational 'Newgate' novels, such as William Harrison Ainsworth's *Jack Sheppard*, which initially outsold *Oliver Twist*. So concerned were the authorities (in the form of the Lord Chamberlain, censor of the stage) that Sheppard's exploits would set a bad example to the youth of England that for 40 years after 1840 no play with the name 'Jack Sheppard' in its title was passed for performance.

'Not less familiar to the people of England is the career of Jack Sheppard, as brutal a ruffian as ever disgraced his country, but who has claims upon the popular admiration which are very generally acknowledged. He did not, like Robin Hood, plunder the rich to relieve the poor, nor rob with an uncouth sort of courtesy, like [Dick] Turpin; but he escaped from Newgate with the fetters on his limbs. This achievement, more than once repeated, has encircled his felon brow with the wreath of immortality ...'

Charles Mackay, *Memoirs of Extraordinary Popular Delusions and the Madness of Crowds* (1841)

PREVIOUS PAGE An engraving after Sir James Thornhill's portrait of the legendary Jack Sheppard.

A sober and orderly boy

The first detailed account of the deeds of Jack Sheppard is *The History of the Remarkable Life of John Sheppard, Containing a Particular Account of His Many Robberies and Escapes*, a ghosted biography published while its subject was still at large. In his opening address 'To the citizens of London and Westminster', the anonymous author – almost certainly Daniel Defoe – is as anxious to deprecate the crimes and misdemeanours of his subject as he is to inflame a prurient interest among his potential readers:

> 'A youth both in age and person, tho' an old man in sin ...'
>
> Daniel Defoe, *The History of the Remarkable Life of John Sheppard* (1724)

> But here's a criminal bids defiance to your laws and justice, who declar'd and has manifested that the bars are not made that can either keep him out, or keep him in, and accordingly hath a second time fled from the very bosom of Death.
>
> His history will astonish! and is not compos'd of fiction, fable, or stories plac'd at York, Rome, or Jamaica, but facts done at your doors, facts unheard of, altogether new, incredible, and yet uncontestable.
>
> He is gone once more upon his wicked range in the world. Restless Vengeance is pursuing, and, gentlemen, 'tis to be hoped that she will be assisted by your endeavours to bring to justice this notorious offender.

The tone of moral indignation might suggest that Sheppard was a serial killer, or at least a violent criminal, but he was no more than a petty thief, a burglar and an occasional dabbler in highway robbery. But this was the 18th century, a period in England when the laws to protect property were at their most draconian, and a man (or woman or boy or girl) could be hanged for the most minor piece of thievery. But Defoe, like journalists ever since, was not averse to earning a quick buck from a sensational tale of true crime. Sheppard's story was also retold in the best-selling *Newgate Calendar*, a compendium of true crime stories that in the 18th century was almost as widely read as the Bible.

Sheppard was born in 1702 in Spitalfields, a poor part of east London. His father, a carpenter, died when he was young, but his mother found him an apprenticeship in his father's trade: 'The lad proved an early proficient, had a ready and ingenious hand,' Defoe writes, 'and had the character of a very sober and orderly boy.' But, before he had finished his seven years' indenture, strong liquor and loose women were to prove Sheppard's undoing. For, the *Newgate Calendar* tells us, 'frequenting the Black Lion ale house in Drury Lane, he became acquainted with some abandoned women, among whom the principal was Elizabeth Lyon, otherwise called 'Edgworth Bess , from the town of Edgworth, where she was born'. Sheppard, besotted, took up with Bess, who by trade was a fence and a pickpocket, and by repute a whore. At the Black Lion he also fell in with a woman known only to history as 'Maggot', who was also a fence – a receiver of stolen goods. It was, the moralizers conclude, under the influence of these jezebels that Sheppard took to stealing tankards, spoons and other items from the houses in which he was employed, and it was at the behest of Maggot that he undertook his first burglary, coming away with goods and money to the value of £22 from the house of a Mr Bains.

A high degree of credit with women of abandoned character

In the last year of his apprenticeship Sheppard left his master and took up with the likes of Joseph 'Blueskins' Blake, James 'Hell and Fury' Sykes and sundry other villains linked to Jonathan Wild – the notorious master criminal known as the Thief-Taker General, on account of his habit of shopping his own associates for the sake of the reward. Sheppard pursued the trade of journeyman carpenter, 'with a view,' the *Newgate Calendar* notes, 'to the easier commission of robbery'. Edgworth Bess, meanwhile, got into trouble with the law, and when Sheppard went to visit her in her place of confinement, according to the *Newgate Calendar*:

> ... the beadle refusing to admit him he knocked him down, broke open the door, and carried her off in triumph – an exploit which acquired him a high degree of credit with the women of abandoned character.

After this, Sheppard and Edgworth Bess were joined in their activities by Sheppard's brother, Thomas, who, for committing two petty offences, had been 'burned in the hand' as punishment. However, Thomas, being apprehended for a break-in in which all three had participated, turned King's evidence and implicated the other two.

'Sheppard was now upon his wicked range in London,' Defoe tells us, 'committing robberies everywhere at discretion.' But there was no honour among thieves, it seems. One day, meeting with 'Hell and Fury' Sykes, the latter invited him to a hostelry near Seven Dials to play a game of skittles. Unbeknownst to Sheppard, Hell and Fury covertly sent for a constable, so pocketing the reward for Sheppard's arrest.

Four escapes ...

Having been brought before a magistrate, Sheppard was confined two storeys up in the roundhouse (the parish lockup) of St Giles. He wasted no time in making an exit. According to Defoe:

> ... 'ere two hours came about, by only the help of a razor and the stretcher of a chair, he broke open the top of the roundhouse, and tying together a sheet and blanket, by them descended into the churchyard and escap'd, leaving the parish to repair the damage, and repent of the affront put upon his skill and capacity.

Shortly after this escape, Sheppard was walking with an associate called Benson across Leicester Fields. The latter having picked a gentleman's pocket for his watch, a hue and cry was got up, and Sheppard was once more apprehended. When Edgworth Bess came to visit him where he was held, in St Anne's roundhouse in

Soho, she too was arrested, and the couple, taken to be man and wife, were committed together to New Prison.

Security was lax, and Sheppard had no difficulty obtaining from his friends who visited him all the items he needed to make his next escape. This came about at two o'clock in the morning of Whitsun Monday, 25 May 1724. According to the *Newgate Calendar*:

> ... he filed off his fetters and, having made a hole in the wall, he took an iron bar and a wooden one out of the window; but as the height from which he was to descend was twenty-five feet he tied a blanket and sheet together, and, making one of them fast to a bar in the window, Edgworth Bess first descended, and Jack followed her. Having reached the yard, they had still a wall of twenty-two feet high to scale; but climbing up by the locks and bolts of the great gate, they got quite out of the prison, and effected a perfect escape.

Like a dog returning to its vomit, Defoe gleefully recounts, Sheppard returned to his wicked ways, and, in cahoots with 'Blueskins' Blake, he proceeded to carry out a number of daring heists, including a touch of highway robbery. But they were betrayed by their fence, a certain William Field: not only did he steal the goods they had invited him to inspect – including 108 yards of woollen cloth stolen from a Mr Kneebone – but he informed on Sheppard and Blueskins to Jonathan Wild, who in turn had them arrested. (Blueskins, who went to the gallows before Sheppard, revenged himself by cutting Wild's throat; the latter survived, but justice, in the person of the hangman, caught up with the Thief-Taker General the following year. Wild's plea that he had brought three score villains to the gallows cut no ice; and the crowd pelted him with rotten fruit as he awaited his end on the scaffold.)

'Next ensued a neglect of Duty, both to God and his master, lying out of nights, perpetual jarrings, and animosities; these and such like, were the consequences of his intimacy with this she Lyon [Elizabeth Lyon, aka Edgworth Bess]; who by the sequel will appear to have been a main loadstone in attracting of him up to this eminence of guilt.'

Daniel Defoe, *The History of the Remarkable Life of John Sheppard* (1724)

Sheppard was held in Newgate Prison, tried, and sentenced to death. His pleas, Defoe tells us, were in vain:

> He begg'd earnestly for transportation, to the most extreme foot of his Majesty's dominions; and pleaded youth and ignorance as the motive which had precipitated him into the guilt; but the Court, deaf to his importunities, as knowing him and his repeated crimes to be equally flagrant, gave him no satisfactory answer. He return'd to his dismal abode, the condemn'd hold ...

On 30 August a warrant was issued for his execution. That same day, he made his third escape, as recounted by the *Newgate Calendar*:

> It is proper to observe that in the old jail of Newgate there was within the lodge a hatch, with large iron spikes, which hatch opened into a dark passage, whence there were a few steps into the condemned hold. The prisoners being permitted to come down to the hatch to speak with their friends, Sheppard, having been supplied with instruments, took an opportunity of cutting one of the spikes in such a manner that it might be easily broken off.
>
> On the evening of the above-mentioned 30th of August, two women of Sheppard's acquaintance [thought to be Edgworth Bess and Maggot] going to visit him, he broke off the spike and, thrusting his head and shoulders through the space, the women pulled him down, and he effected his escape, notwithstanding some of the keepers were at that time drinking at the other end of the lodge.

> **Sheppard's fame was greatly celebrated among the lower order of people by this exploit.**
>
> The Newgate Calendar, referring to Sheppard's second escape

It was not long, however, before the keepers of Newgate caught up with Sheppard. His plan to go to ground in the country had come to naught, and he returned instead to his old drinking haunts around the city. But after a close shave with a sheriff's officer in Drury Lane, Sheppard left London for Finchley, and it was here, following the receipt of 'many intelligences' as to his whereabouts, that he was apprehended once more. 'The joy the people of Newgate conceiv'd on this occasion is inexpressible,' Defoe writes. '*Te Deum* was sung in the Lodge, and nothing but smiles, and bumpers [tankards filled to brim and raised in a toast], were seen there for many days together.'

This time the turnkeys took no chances. Sheppard was locked in a strong room known as the Castle, handcuffed, loaded with a heavy pair of leg irons, and chained to a staple fixed in the floor. Now he was a celebrity, he received visits from great numbers of people of all ranks. 'Scarce anyone,' the *Newgate Calendar* observes, 'left him without making him a present in money, though he would have more gladly received a file, a hammer, or a chisel; but the utmost care was taken that none of his visitors should furnish him with such implements.'

Without such implements, he had to fall back on his own ingenuity. On 15 October, when the keepers and their assistants were expected to attend the

> **The concourse of people of tolerable fashion to see him was exceeding great; he was always cheerful and pleasant to a degree, as turning almost everything as was said into a jest and banter.**
>
> Daniel Defoe, *The History of the Remarkable Life of John Sheppard* (1724), on Sheppard's many prison visitors prior to his fourth escape

sessions at the Old Bailey, he made his bid for freedom. His handcuffs came off without difficulty, and a nail proved the ideal tool to unpick the padlock linking the chain to the staple in the floor. He hid his leg irons under his stockings, making them fast with his garters, then squeezed up the chimney to the room above, having forcibly removed an iron bar that blocked the way. The door of the room above was locked, but in seven minutes he had broken through. Several more locked doors had to be negotiated, but Sheppard opened them all, using a combination of brute force and guile. At nine o'clock in the evening he was once more in the open air. He was still high above the ground, however, and had to use his blanket tied onto his stockings to lower himself onto the roof of an adjoining house. The door to the garret of the house was open, and he softly stole down two flights of stairs and out into the street. Somewhere a woman, hearing the clinking of his chains, inquired 'What noise is that?' 'Only a dog or a cat,' a man reassured her.

It was a prodigious effort. 'Infinite numbers of citizens,' Defoe tells us, 'came to Newgate to behold Sheppard's workmanship.' All agreed that the great escape owed nothing to the negligence or connivance of the turnkeys, and everything to the ingenuity and perseverance of the unrepentant young villain.

... and a hanging

When Defoe published his account, Sheppard was still at large. But not for long. For a couple of nights he took shelter in a disused cowshed in the fields near Tottenham Court. The offer of 20 shillings secured the services of a shoemaker, who freed the fugitive of his leg irons, and then, ripping his clothes and disguising himself as a beggar, Sheppard wandered the public houses, delighting in hearing his audacious deeds broadcast by the ballad singers. But the guise of a beggar offended his *amour propre*, so, to mend his pride, he broke into a pawnbroker's premises in Drury Lane and equipped himself with all the accoutrements of a gentleman – black suit, ruffled shirt, tie-wig, silver-hilted sword, snuffbox, gold watch and diamond ring.

> ... when any nobleman came to see him he never failed to beg that they would intercede with the King for a pardon, to which he thought that his singular dexterity gave him some pretensions.

The *Newgate Calendar* describes Sheppard's last period in prison prior to his execution

On 31 October, emboldened in his finery, Sheppard dined with two women in Newgate Street and drove in a coach past the prison itself. That evening, becoming sentimental, he invited his mother to share a bottle of brandy with him. She implored him to flee the country, but the drink made him foolish, and he employed the time until midnight in wandering from inn to tavern to public house. He was recognized,

ABOVE William Hogarth's engraving of the 'Idle 'Prentice Executed at Tyburn', the penultimate plate of *Industry and Idleness*. Hogarth's series, published in 1747, was partly inspired by the career and fate of Jack Sheppard.

'What amazing difficulties has he overcome! what astonishing things has he performed! and all for the sake of a stinking, miserable carcass; hardly worth the hanging!'

Extract from the sermon of a street preacher, using Sheppard as an example of the great care men take in looking after their bodies, and the great neglect they bestow upon their souls; quoted by the Reverend Mr Villette, the editor of the *Annals of Newgate* (1754)

and reported, and when, as the clocks struck twelve, he was taken into custody one last time, he was quite senseless with the quantity and variety of liquors he had consumed.

Sheppard seems to have assumed that his newfound celebrity status, following his multiple escapes, would ensure him a pardon. This was not to be. His death sentence was reiterated on 10 November, after he refused to name

his associates in exchange for a commutation. The day of his execution was fixed for the following Monday, 16 November. When the day came, a search of his person found a penknife, with which he had apparently planned to cut his bonds as he was transported to the gallows, with the idea of making a run for it and disappearing amongst the crowds. This ruse having failed, he had already arranged a contingency plan with his friends (possibly with Defoe himself, who would have been loath to lose such an asset). The plan was that after he had been hanged by his neck for the customary 15 minutes and cut down, he would then be taken to a warm bed and revived by opening a vein – a ruse that appears to have worked in other cases. (In 1740, for example, a man called William Duell, hanged for murder, was about to be dissected by students at Surgeons Hall when he gave signs of life; his sentence was commuted to transportation.)

Some 200,000 people turned out to watch Jack Sheppard's procession from Newgate to the gallows tree at Tyburn, accompanied by the city marshal and the liveried Javelin Men, while scores of women, dressed in white, strewed flowers in his path. It was a scene subsequently satirized by Gay in *The Beggar's Opera*, in which Mrs Peachum avers that 'Women ... are so partial to the brave that they think every man handsome who is going to the camp or the gallows.' She then launches into song:

THE TYBURN TREE

MOST PUBLIC EXECUTIONS IN LONDON were carried out in the district of Tyburn, close to where Marble Arch now stands. The first hanging took place here in 1388, and in 1571 a permanent gallows was erected – the infamous 'Tyburn Tree', a large, three-cornered affair capable of dispatching 21 people at once. The last hanging at Tyburn took place in 1783; thereafter, executions were carried out at Newgate Prison.

Many slang terms came to be associated with Tyburn. *To dance the Tyburn jig*, for example, was to be hanged; *to preach at Tyburn cross* meant the same thing; while a *Tyburn blossom* was, according to Francis Grose's *Classical Dictionary of the Vulgar Tongue* (1796), 'a young thief or pickpocket, who in time will ripen into fruit borne by the deadly never-green [i.e. the Tyburn Tree]'. Such was the opprobrium thus associated with Tyburn that the district eventually renamed itself Marylebone.

> Beneath the left ear so fit but a cord,
> (A rope so charming a zone is!)
> The youth in his cart hath the air of a lord,
> And we cry, 'There dies an Adonis!'

At a tavern in Oxford Street the cavalcade stopped so that Sheppard could down one last pint of sack, while at Tyburn itself, copies of Defoe's 'official' biography were on sale – although missing one final chapter. 'He behaved with great decency at the place of execution,' the *Newgate Calendar* avers, but adds, 'He died with difficulty, and was much pitied by the surrounding multitude.' Some reports suggest the crowd rushed forward to pull on his legs, to shorten his agony as he slowly strangled to death; others suggest they only got hold of him once he was cut down, determined to preserve his body from the indignity of post-mortem dissection by the anatomists. In either case, the plan to resuscitate Jack Sheppard and restore him to the land of the living was foiled, and that evening the young wonder was laid to rest in the churchyard of St Martin-in-the-Fields, in the very heart of London. It may have been of some consolation to Defoe that his client had left the field at the top of his game. Too much success too young has spoilt many a celebrity career, and glamour and youthful good looks rarely survive the siren calls of the gambling den, the gin shop and the bordello.

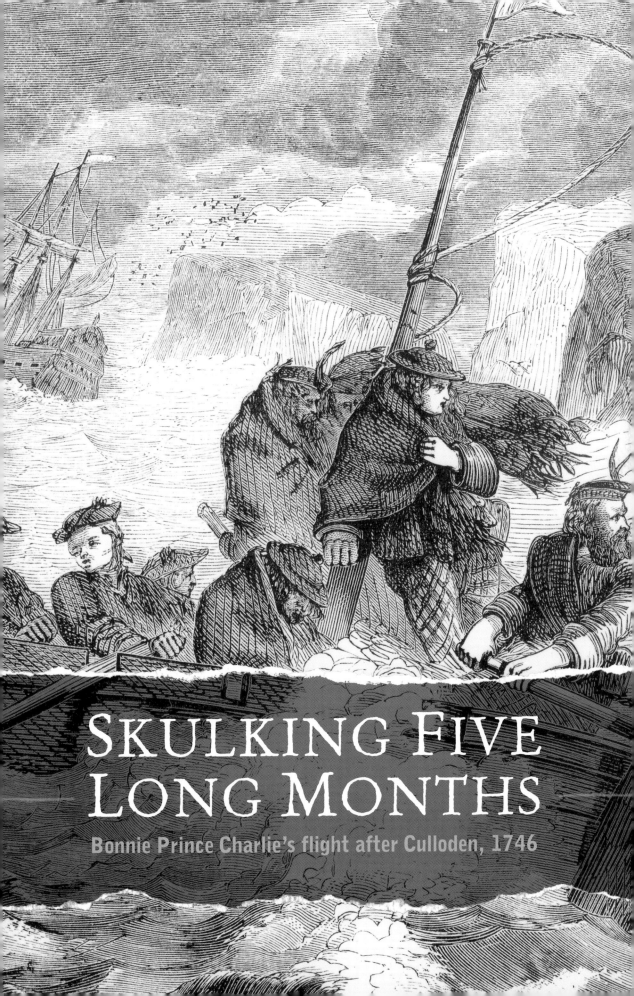

Skulking Five Long Months

Bonnie Prince Charlie's flight after Culloden, 1746

On 16 April 1746 an army of well-drilled Hanoverian Redcoats faced a smaller Jacobite force on a bleak stretch of moorland east of Inverness. The place was called Culloden Muir. A sharp wind blew and a steady rain fell as the Duke of Cumberland, younger son of King George II and commander of the government forces, addressed his troops: 'Depend, my lads, on your bayonets; let them mingle with you; let them know the men they have to deal with.'

On the rebel side there was dissension among the commanders, whose army consisted of Highland clansmen sent hither by their chiefs, backed up by a few French regulars. Lord George Murray was angry with Colonel John O'Sullivan for his choice of ground on which to take on the enemy. The open moor, he said, was 'not proper for Highlanders'. The man they were fighting for, Prince Charles Edward Stuart, backed O'Sullivan. It was a disastrous decision.

The battle began at 1 p.m. The Highlanders charged 'like troops of hungry wolves', but proved no match for the Hanoverian artillery, nor the disciplined rows of Redcoats, who held their ground. It was all over in 40 minutes, and, according to one contemporary account, 'the soldiers' bayonets were stain'd and clotted with the blood of the rebels up to the muzzles of their muskets'. The last land battle on British soil turned into a rout, putting an end to Jacobite hopes of a Stuart restoration. As Cumberland's dragoons set about slaughtering any fleeing or wounded Highlander they came across, O'Sullivan told the prince that 'all was going to pot', and that he should save himself. The dashing, gallant – and fundamentally foolish – young man known to his swooning admirers as Bonnie Prince Charlie thus became a fugitive with a price of £30,000 on his head. So began five months of wandering, as the pretender who had laid claim to the throne of Great Britain and Ireland set off into the wilds of the Highlands to evade the pursuing Redcoats.

> *Weep, Albin, to death and captivity led.*
> *Oh weep, but thy tears cannot number the dead:*
> *For a merciless sword on Culloden shall wave,*
> *Culloden, that reeks with the blood of the brave.*

Thomas Campbell, 'Lochiel's Warning'

Into the wild

The defeat had come so rapidly that the Jacobites had no proper contingency plans. The prince himself headed for Fort Augustus, at the southwest end of Loch Ness, which had been mentioned as a possible reassembly point for his scattered

PREVIOUS PAGE During the course of his wanderings, Bonnie Prince Charlie made several voyages in open boats across the perilous seas of the Hebrides.

army. On the way he stopped at Gortleck House, where he was given a guarded welcome by Lord Lovat, the Fraser chief known as Simon the Fox, who had supported both Hanoverians and Jacobites over the years and who had hedged his bets by sending his son to fight for the prince while he himself stayed at home. Lovat, it is said, welcomed the prince with a glass of wine and sent him on his way after two more. (This did not save his neck: found guilty of treason, Lovat was beheaded on Tower Hill in London on 9 April 1747, the last man in Britain to suffer this fate.)

When the prince reached Fort Augustus, he found that the clans had failed to rally there. Pressing on down the Great Glen, he arrived at Invergarry early on the morning of 17 April. He and his small party rested until mid-afternoon, before heading further down the Great Glen, past Loch Lochy. They then turned westward into the mountainous wilderness.

The going eventually got so rough that the prince and his small party had to abandon their horses. Exhausted, the prince slept through much of one day in a remote cottage in a wood, before walking by moonlight through Arisaig to the west coast and the shores of Loch nan Uamh – where, just nine months before, he had landed from the French brig *Du Teillay* to launch his bid for the throne. Now the prince intended to get back to France as soon as he could, persuading himself – as he abandoned his Highland supporters to their fate – that he could do his own cause more good by urging the French to participate in a large-scale invasion (which, despite earlier promises, had hitherto failed to materialize).

The problem was to get a ship. He hoped that the great chiefs of Skye, MacLeod of Dunvegan and Macdonald of Sleat, would provide him with assistance, but was told that they had turned their coats and were actively hunting for him. By a stroke of luck, the Hanoverians had heard a report that the prince had fled to the remote islands of St Kilda, far out in the Atlantic, 50 miles (80 km) beyond the Western Isles. Thus all the available ships of the Royal Navy were diverted there, giving the prince the opportunity to slip across the Minch to the Outer Hebrides.

> 'For a prince to be a-skulking five long months exposed to the hardships of hunger and cold, thirst and nakedness, and surrounded on all hands by a numerous army of bloodthirsty men, both by sea and land, eagerly hunting after the price of blood, and yet that they should miss the much coveted aim, is an event of life far surpassing the power of words to paint.'

Bishop Robert Forbes, *The Lyon in Mourning*. This collection of speeches, journals, letters and eyewitness accounts pertaining to Prince Charles Edward Stuart and the '45 Rising was collected by Forbes, a Jacobite sympathizer, between 1746 and 1775, and eventually published in 1895. It is the main source for the wanderings of the prince after Culloden.

Across the Minch

On the night of 26 April the prince embarked in an eight-oared open boat skippered by the 68-year-old Donald MacLeod of Gualtergill, a man renowned for his skills as a pilot. The prince had heard of this man, and had sought him out on the shore of Arisaig. 'I am in distress,' he told him, 'I therefore throw myself upon your bosom, and let you do with me what you like.' Donald had predicted a storm, and advised against putting out to sea, but the prince was adamant – and equally adamant, once the wind and the rain began to buffet them, that they should turn back, 'For,' he said, 'I had rather face cannons and muskets than be drowned in such a storm as this.' But the old sailor, who later said he had never trysted with such a tempest before, insisted it was impossible to turn into the wind and land safely on the rocky shore of Arisaig. 'Why,' Donald explained, 'since we are here we have nothing for it, but, under God, to set out to sea directly. Is it not as good for us to be drown'd in clean water as to be dashed to pieces upon a rock and be drown'd too?' That quietened the passengers, who, according to Donald, were 'expecting every moment to be overwhelmed with the violence of the waves, and to sink to the bottom'.

> Sing me a song of a lad that is gone,
> Say, could that lad be I?
> Merry of soul he sailed on a day
> Over the sea to Skye.
>
> Robert Louis Stevenson: 'Sing me a song of a lad that is gone', from *Songs of Travel* (1896)

So they passed through the Cuillin Sound between the islands of Skye and Rum, and out into the Minch, the notoriously stormy stretch of sea between the Inner and Outer Hebrides. Raising sail, they made good speed before the southeasterly gale, although 'they had neither pump nor compass nor lantern with them, and the night turned so pitch dark that they knew not where they were for the most of the course'. After eight hours they had covered a distance of more than 60 miles (100 km), and, as Donald put it, 'by peep of day we discovered ourselves to be on the coast of the Long Isle [i.e. the long chain of the Outer Hebrides], and we made directly to the nearest land, which was Rushness in the Island Benbecula'.

For two months Donald piloted the prince up and down the length of the Long Isle, to Harris and Lewis in the north, and then back down to North Uist, Benbecula and South Uist. All this time they played a desperate game of hide-and-seek with their pursuers. A force of Redcoats under General Campbell had landed on Barra to the south, and were working their way northward, while the ships of the Royal Navy, back from their wild goose chase to St Kilda, were patrolling the seas of the Hebrides, on constant lookout for French vessels come to take the prince to safety. As the Jacobite officer Captain Alexander MacDonald – better known to posterity as the great Gaelic poet Alasdair MacMaighstir Alasdair – later reported, the prince and his small retinue were 'now encompassed by no less than three or four thousand bloody hounds, by sea and land, thirsting for the captivity and noble blood of their Prince'.

Over the sea to Skye

It is at this point that Flora MacDonald, a young lady from South Uist, enters the story. Charles's advisers hit upon the stratagem of dressing the prince as Miss MacDonald's Irish servant, one Betty Burke, so that he might cross the Minch to Skye in her company. 'At first the young woman was surprised,' Alexander MacDonald recalled, 'but then when spoke to sincerely did condescend to go with his royal highness through the vast world if it should contribute in the least to his safety.'

Thus the prince found himself dressed in a calico gown, a quilted petticoat, a mantle of tough waterproof cloth, a cap, women's shoes – and stockings. He desired to secrete a pistol in his petticoat, but Flora vetoed the idea, saying if they were searched, the discovery of the pistol would give the game away. The prince retorted that if the search were that close, they would 'certainly discover me at any rate'. However, he agreed to settle for a short, heavy cudgel, 'with which he design'd to do his best to knock down any single person that should attack him'.

Thus disguised, in late June the prince embarked from Benbecula in a 15-foot (4.5 m) ketch with Flora and four oarsmen. The weather was no better than when the prince had crossed the Minch in April: 'Hard gales and squally weather' was the entry in the log of HMS *Raven*, just one of several Royal Navy vessels patrolling the Minch on the lookout for the prince. To add to the discomfort, the wind was joined by a drenching downpour much to Flora's distress. The Young Chevalier now acted the gallant, a part he always played prettily, singing the young lady to sleep while her head rested in his hands.

It was a long and weary voyage, not without its alarms. At one point they were becalmed in a thick fog, at another point, as they passed the northern shores of Skye, they were spotted by a group of soldiers who raised a shout, but, as the prince's boat

ANOTHER JACOBITE IN DRAG

AFTER THE ABORTIVE JACOBITE REBELLION OF 1715, William Maxwell, 5th Earl of Nithsdale, found himself imprisoned in the Tower of London, having been captured by Hanoverian forces in the wake of the defeat at Preston. Found guilty of treason, he was sentenced to death, but the day before he was due to be executed, 24 February 1716, he received a visit from his countess who dressed him in the clothes of her serving maid, and so smuggled him out of the Tower to safety. The couple lived out their days in contented penury in Rome. Lord Nithsdale's fellows were not so fortunate: the day after his escape Viscount Kenmure and the Earl of Derwentwater were beheaded on Tower Hill.

made no haste to escape, their suspicions appear to have dissipated. One government vessel recorded in its log a small unidentified boat close to the shore. Eventually, after nearly three days at sea, they made landfall on Skye.

The island was thick with Redcoats, so Flora and the prince avoided the trodden ways and made their way across the bogs and burns of the Trotternish peninsula to a safe house, that of MacDonald of Kingsburgh. There the appearance of Miss Burke alarmed the womenfolk. Kingsburgh's daughter was affrighted by this 'very odd, muckle [large], ill-shaken-up wife', while his wife was shocked by the sight of the 'odd muckle trallup of a carlin [witch, old hag] making lang, wide steps through the hall', and even more shocked when Miss Burke, who had not shaved for days, gave her a kiss. Kingsburgh explained to his confused spouse that she had the honour of the prince in her house. 'The Prince!' she cried, 'O Lord, we are a' ruin'd and undone forever! We will a' be hang'd now!' Her husband sought to reassure her that they all had to die some time, 'and if we are hanged for this, I am sure we will die in a good cause'.

> 'Speed, bonnie boat, like a bird on the wing, 'Onward,' the sailors cry; Carry the lad that's born to be king, Over the sea to Skye.'
>
> Harold Edwin Boulton, 'The Skye Boat Song' (1908)

Highland hospitality

More adventures followed. Crossing back to the mainland in early July, the prince traversed the Rough Bounds of Knoydart – still one of the wildest stretches of country in Britain – evading the cordon of Redcoat camps and patrols. He continued north over the mountains, hoping for a French ship at Poolewe, but his hopes were dashed when he heard that such a vessel had come and gone.

Just as the prince's fortunes seemed at a low ebb, he encountered a group of impoverished outlaws, a group known ever since as the Seven Men of Glen Moriston. These 'broken men' had served in the prince's army, and were now obliged to fend for themselves in the wilderness. The Seven Men, spurning the temptation of the £30,000 reward, hid the prince in their hut, and then in a cave further up the hillside, where he was 'as comfortably lodged as if he had been in a royal palace', and feasted on mutton, venison, butter, cheese and whisky. Meanwhile, an Edinburgh merchant and Jacobite sympathizer called Roderick Mackenzie was travelling through Glen Moriston, and was mistaken by some Redcoats for the royal fugitive. Shot and fatally wounded, Mackenzie maintained the deception, crying, 'Alas, you have killed your Prince!' His severed head was taken to Fort Augustus, where the Duke of Cumberland was convinced he had his man, so helping the real prince make good his escape.

The prince headed south once more, having heard from his faithful follower Cameron of Lochiel, who had been badly wounded at Culloden, that he would be safe if he joined him in his hiding place, while other trusted men kept a watch on the west coast for French ships. The prince eventually met up with Lochiel beside Loch Ericht, in the midst of another wild tract of the Highlands, beneath the slopes of remote Ben Alder. They subsequently became the guests of another fugitive chief, Ewan Macpherson of Cluny, who had built himself a shelter further up the slopes of the mountain. This structure, known as Cluny's Cage, is recreated in Robert Louis Stevenson's *Kidnapped* (1886), a story set in the aftermath of the '45 Rising:

> Quite at the top, and just before the rocky face of the cliff sprang above the foliage, we found that strange house which was known in the country as 'Cluny's Cage'. The trunks of several trees had been wattled across, the intervals strengthened with stakes, and the ground behind this barricade levelled up with earth to make the floor. A tree, which grew out from the hillside, was the living centre-beam of the roof. The walls were of wattle and covered with moss. The whole house had something of an egg shape; and it half hung, half stood in that steep, hillside thicket, like a wasp's nest in a green hawthorn.

Compared to sleeping in the heather wrapped in a plaid, it was luxury, and the prince gorged himself on sausages, ham and pans of minced collops, all washed down with plentiful draughts of whisky.

Then word came that a French frigate had been seen off the coast of Arisaig. Four successive night marches took them west to Loch nan Uamh, where the prince had first landed in Scotland 14 months before, and from where he had embarked for Benbecula a few days after Culloden. On 19 September, accompanied by Lochiel, he boarded the frigate, the happily named *L'Heureux*. Before midnight they had set sail for France.

The varied fates of the rebels

Reprisals against those who had helped the prince were savage. Lord Lovat, as has been recorded, lost his head on Tower Hill; Lords Kilmarnock and Balmerino, who had fought at Culloden, met the same fate before him, the former offering to defy precedence by inviting the latter, a peer of inferior rank, to be the first to lay his head on the block (this gallant gesture was ignored by the sheriffs). Many others, if they were not hanged, were imprisoned in hulks on the Thames, in what Bishop Forbes called a 'deplorable state of misery, their clothes wearing off

'We'll o'er the water, we'll o'er the sea,
We'll o'er the water to Charlie;
Come weel, come wo, we'll gather
 and go,
And live or die wi' Charlie.'

James Hogg, 'O'er the Water to Charlie', from *Jacobite Relics of Scotland*, Second Series (1821)

ABOVE Bonnie Prince Charlie wearing his trademark tartan trews. In his bonnet can be seen a white rose, the emblem of the House of Stuart worn by supporters of the Jacobite cause.

Bonnie Chairlie's noo awa',
Safely ower the friendly main;
Mony a heart will break in twa',
Should he ne'er come back again.

Chorus:
Will ye no come back again?
Will ye no come back again?
Better lo'ed ye canna be,
Will ye no come back again?

Ye trusted in your Hielan' men,
They trusted you dear Chairlie.
They kent your hidin' in the glen,
Death or exile bravin'.

[*Chorus*]

We watched thee in the gloamin' hour,
We watched thee in the mornin' grey.
Tho' thirty thousand pounds they gie,
O there is nane that wad betray.

[*Chorus*]

Sweet the laverock' s note and lang,
Liltin' wildly up the glen.
But aye tae me he sings ae sang,
Will ye no' come back again?

[*Chorus*]

Lady Nairne (1766–1845), 'Will Ye No' Come Back Again?'
(gloamin' = dusk; laverock = lark)

them so that many of them had not a single rag to cover their nakedness'. Large numbers died in these appalling conditions. The boatmen who had helped the prince escape had confessions beaten out of them, but no one ever claimed the £30,000 reward. When asked about this, Donald MacLeod, who had piloted the prince across the Minch, told his interrogator, General Campbell:

> What then? thirty thousand pounds! Though I had gotten it I could not have enjoyed it eight and forty hours. Conscience would have gotten up upon me. That money could not have kept it down. And tho' I could have gotten all England and Scotland for my pains I would not allow a hair of his body to be touch'd if I could help it.

General Campbell, although belonging to the clan most devoted to the Hanoverian cause, was impressed: 'I will not say you are in the wrong,' he said.

Flora MacDonald, the heroine of the tale, was arrested when her role in the prince's escape became clear. She was dispatched south as a prisoner, but was treated well, and was released under the 1747 Act of Indemnity. In 1750 she married Allan MacDonald of Kingsburgh. Many years later, in 1773, Dr Johnson, something of a Jacobite at heart, met Flora at her home on Skye, a circumstance that made his companion, James Boswell, pause for thought – as he recorded in his *Journal of a Tour to the Hebrides*:

> She was a little woman of mild and genteel appearance, mighty soft and well-bred. To see Mr Samuel Johnson salute Miss Flora MacDonald was a wonderful romantic scene to me ... To see Mr Samuel Johnson lying in Prince Charles's bed, in the Isle of Skye, in the house of Miss Flora MacDonald, struck me with such a group of ideas as it is not easy for words to describe as the mind perceives them.

For his part, Dr Johnson opined that Flora MacDonald was 'a name that will be mentioned in history, and if courage and fidelity be virtues, mentioned with honour'.

For a time after the prince's departure, there were those who lived in hope of a Stuart restoration. Before he left Scotland, Charles had asked Cluny to remain in order to prepare for his return, and so the Macpherson chief spent another eight years in his Cage, fruitlessly waiting. The French king never was persuaded to support a second landing, and the remaining four decades of the prince's life, after his year or so of high adventure, turned into a sad, drink-sodden disappointment. By the time of his death in 1788 his claim to the throne of Great Britain and Ireland was not recognized by a single European sovereign. In Scotland itself, meanwhile, the old clan system and its Gaelic culture was on its way to extinction, and the Jacobite cause had petered out into nothing more than a mist of sentimental songs and romantic yearnings.

IMPRISONED BY A MOST DETESTABLE TYRANNY

Casanova breaks out of the Doge's Palace, 1756

Few would have heard of the strange and varied career of
the 18th-century diplomat, spy and philanderer Giacomo
Casanova had he not, in his old age, written *The Story of My
Life*, an engrossing account not just of his own numerous
amorous conquests, but also of the manners and mores of high
society in the twilight days of Europe's *anciens régimes*. A
native of Venice, Casanova spent much of his life wandering the
capitals of Europe, gambling, charming and seducing as he went.
Needless to say, such a rackety lifestyle not infrequently got him
into trouble, and in 1755 he found himself thrown into prison in
his native city, for reasons that were never made clear. His
account of his escape after 15 months incarceration may owe
something to his talent for self-dramatization, but the nub of the
tale is certainly true, and the damage he caused during his prison
break is scrupulously recorded in the Venetian state archives.

Casanova – whose very name has become inextricably linked with devil-may-care
libertinage – must have been a disappointment to his parents, both of whom were
involved in the theatre, but wished for their son the more respectable career of
ecclesiastical lawyer. At the age of 12 young Casanova was packed off to the
University of Padua to read law, for which he had, he said, an 'unconquerable
aversion'. He also studied moral philosophy, chemistry and mathematics, but his real,
albeit thwarted, vocation was medicine, and
he remained fascinated by the workings and
frailties of the human body and the human
mind for the rest of his life.

> I should have been allowed to
> do as I wished and become a
> physician, in which profession
> quackery is even more effective
> than it is in legal practice.
>
> Giacomo Casanova, *The Story of My Life*

After graduating at the age of 17,
Casanova took minor orders as an abbé, and
began his career in ecclesiastical law. But he
did not adopt the sober garb of a lawyer,
cultivating instead the mien and flashy dress
of a dandy. Under the tutelage of his first patron, an elderly Venetian senator, he
came to appreciate the good things of life – fine food, fine wine and beautiful women
– but before long he found himself dogged by gambling debts and scandals, resulting
in a short spell in prison. On his release he swapped an ecclesiastical career for a
military one, only to find the routine dull and advancement slow. A bid to become a
professional gambler ended quickly when he lost all his money, and for a while he
tried his hand as a journeyman violinist. Salvation came in the form of another rich

PREVIOUS PAGE Casanova's daring escape over the roof of his prison in Venice.

patron, Senator Bragadin, who employed Casanova as a legal assistant and shared with him his interest in the esoteric teachings of cabalism, until further scandals forced the younger man to depart from Venice once more. Embarking on the Grand Tour, Casanova continued his amatory exploits, became a Freemason, and spent two years in Paris, eventually returning to Venice in 1753.

Venetians first, Christians second

Venice was then the capital of worldly voluptuousness, where the young men of Europe flocked to consort with the masked but easy-going ladies – of whom it was said that they were Venetians first and Christians second. Indeed, many of these women were technically nuns, confined in convents not out of a sense of vocation, but because their families wanted their honour protected until they could be married to a suitable man, or because they were not, for dynastic reasons, to be married at all. The British ambassador in the 1750s, John Murray, claimed that any nun in Venice could be had 'for a hundred sequins', and few seem to have cavilled at embarking on affairs – although these amours had to be kept discreet, given the stern outward conservatism of the Venetian state.

Casanova had affairs with two such women. The first, identified in his memoirs as CC, was a young lady with whom he seems to have genuinely fallen in love, and whom he determined to make pregnant in order to overcome her family's

ABOVE *The Visiting Parlour in the Convent*, by Pietro Longhi. Casanova found that the ladies who resided in the convents of Venice were far from chaste – a discovery that may have led, indirectly, to his imprisonment.

> **My libertine ways could at worst make me guilty to myself ...**
>
> Giacomo Casanova, *The Story of My Life*

opposition to their getting married. However, they instead sent her off to a convent, where (according to Casanova) she succumbed to the charms of an older nun, identified as MM, who invited Casanova to have an affair with her in lieu. MM was already the mistress of the French ambassador, the worldly Cardinal de Bernis (a man in his late thirties), but he actively encouraged her to take other lovers, and approved of Casanova, a fellow Freemason. A febrile *ménage à trois* and even *à quatre* then ensued, according to Casanova's memoirs, which reveal the unfolding complexities of *ces affaires* in a succession of dialogues, epistolary exchanges and steamy tableaux that may owe more to the conventions of contemporary pornography and novels of sensibility than the historical truth.

Nevertheless, the affairs were real enough for the Venetian authorities to take note. As far as they were concerned, Casanova's sin was not that MM was a nun, but that she was from a wealthy patrician family, and Casanova, the actor's son, had therefore trespassed across the class divide. The fact that he was losing MM's money at the gaming tables also raised eyebrows. It was not just his affairs that gave offence. His choice of drinking companions displeased the close-knit Venetian oligarchy, who did not like their sons consorting with seditious radicals – which is how they viewed Casanova, on the grounds of his Freemasonry, his adherence to the cabbala, and his generally disrespectful carryings-on. Among the young blades with whom Casanova consorted were the three Memmo brothers, Andrea, Bernardo and Lorenzo, scions of an ancient Venetian house. Their mother accused Casanova of corrupting her boys and blamed

> **I varied our pleasures in a thousand different ways, and I astonished her by making her feel that she was susceptible of greater enjoyment than she had any idea of.**
>
> Giacomo Casanova, *The Story of My Life*, describing his first night with the nun known as MM, who had come to him masked, and dressed as a man

him for their gambling debts. Members of the family of Senator Bragadin, Casanova's patron, were also unhappy with Casanova's supposed influence over their elderly relative, and blamed the younger man for turning the senator against a proposed marriage.

A bulky dossier was secretly compiled by the three-man Inquisitori di Stato, the body concerned with internal security in the Serene Republic. They concluded that Casanova was 'a man with a tendency to hyperbole who manages to live at the expense of this or that person on the strength of his lies or his ability to cheat'. There were also many who found Casanova's opinionated outbursts on literary, religious and ecclesiastical matters offensive (atheism was suspected), while others sneered that his frequent seductions were merely a means to social and financial advancement – a slur that Casanova, in his memoirs, did all he could to refute, depicting himself as a man of exquisite sensibility, drawn into his amorous adventures by a too tender heart, and repenting when his sexual appetites sometimes led him to excess.

The first clear sign of the Establishment's displeasure came when the chief of police arrived at Casanova's rooms to search for contraband salt. Casanova expressed his outrage to Bragadin, who advised the younger man to calm down and treat the police visit as a warning. He should leave Venice at once. But Casanova, not realizing the danger he was in, defiantly stayed put.

> 'The next day, however, when I came to think of that rather too lively night, during which, as is generally the case, Love had routed Reason, I felt some remorse.'
>
> Giacomo Casanova, *The Story of My Life*, referring to his first *ménage à trois* with MM and CC

Over the Bridge of Sighs

When, on 26 July 1755, the Inquisition arrived at his rooms to arrest him, they brought with them three dozen men-at-arms, leading Casanova to observe:

> It is curious that in London, where everyone is brave, only one man is needed to arrest another, whereas in my dear native land, where cowardice prevails, thirty are required.

Searching his rooms, they found plenty more evidence to incriminate their man: for Casanova's library contained many of the books listed in the Vatican's *Index Librorum Prohibitorum*, damned on the grounds of free-thinking, occultism, indecency or sacrilege.

Ever the debonair *homme du monde*, Casanova took his time at his toilette, shaved himself, combed his hair, and dressed himself in his holiday suit. But underneath his calm surface he was in a state of shock, and admitted that after his arrest he was obliged to pass water every quarter of an hour, a circumstance that lead him to conclude, in a spirit of scientific detachment, that 'great surprise is also a diuretic'.

Casanova was taken by gondola along a maze of small canals to the Grand Canal and the Prigioni Nuove, the New Prison, and from thence across the closed bridge known as the Ponte dei Sospiri, the Bridge of Sighs, for few prisoners who crossed it ever returned alive. The bridge led to the Doge's Palace and the infamous prison of the Inquisition, Il Piombi, the Leads, so called because it was situated just under the lead roof of the palace. On his way to his cell, Casanova passed through the Inquisitors' meeting room, on whose walls hung Hieronymous Bosch's terrifying depictions of Hell. From there he was taken up another flight of stairs and came to a dirty, rat-infested garret, where his jailer delighted in pointing out to him the machine used to garrotte condemned prisoners.

The cells of Il Piombi lay on either side of the garret, and the lead roof meant that in

> 'Nature, when a man listens to her and nothing else, takes him from one folly to another, till she puts him under the Leads.'
>
> Giacomo Casanova, *The Story of My Life*

winter the prison was freezing cold and in summer roasting hot. Each cell measured some eight by ten feet, but was only five feet high, so most men had to stoop. The humiliation and discomfort of the prisoners was reinforced by the fact that the doors to the cells were only three feet high, forcing them to crawl into captivity. The only light came dimly through the grating in the door, and the only furniture was a bench and a bucket.

Casanova was never told of the charges against him. There was no trial, the Inquisition merely noting in its records the following:

> Having taken cognizance of the grave faults committed by G. Casanova primarily in public outrages against the holy religion, their Excellencies have caused him to be arrested and imprisoned under the Leads.

Casanova had no idea how long he was to be confined, initially hoping that it would only be for a day or two, as a kind of smack on the wrist. In fact, he had been sentenced to five years.

On the edge of madness

For eight hours Casanova remained in a trance, not moving, not even thinking. No one brought him anything to eat or drink, not even bread and water. Eventually hunger and thirst roused him from his torpor:

> When I heard eight o'clock strike I became furious, knocking at the door, stamping my feet, fretting and fuming, and accompanying this useless hubbub with loud cries. After more than an hour of this wild exercise, seeing no one, without the slightest reason to think I could be heard, and shrouded in darkness, I shut the grating for fear of the rats, and threw myself at full length upon the floor.

In his despair he came to the conclusion that the Inquisition intended to starve him to death, but, like a character in a Kafka novel, he could think of no crime he had committed that could warrant such a fate.

Eventually, exhausted, he fell asleep. Waking at midnight, he reached out his hand to find his handkerchief, only to feel beside him a hand as cold as ice. Terrified, he fell

> I came to the conclusion that the Inquisitors had sworn my death. My investigation as to what I had done to deserve such a fate was not a long one, for in the most scrupulous examination of my conduct I could find no crimes. I was, it is true, a profligate, a gambler, a bold talker, a man who thought of little besides enjoying this present life, but in all that there was no offence against the state.

Giacomo Casanova, *The Story of My Life*

into a swoon, incapable of comprehension, then, recovering his senses, reached out again – only to touch the frozen hand once more. 'This is the body of a strangled wretch,' he told himself, 'and they would thus warn me of the fate which is in store for me.' With this thought, fear turned to rage, and with rage came determination, and for a third time he stretched out his hand – only to find that he had in his grasp his own left hand, which, pressed under the weight of his body on the hard floor, had gone completely numb. Rather than seeing the funny side, Casanova plunged into the darkest fancies:

> I saw that I was in a place where, if the false appeared true, the truth might appear false, where understanding was bereaved of half its prerogatives, where the imagination becoming affected would either make the reason a victim to empty hopes or to dark despair.

Casanova, a creature of the Enlightenment, tried to summon reason to his aid, but found that only wrath answered his call. In his fury he imagined the bloody revenge he would wreak upon his persecutors, upon the government of the Serene Republic itself, when he was released in the morning – as he surely would be.

At half-past four, in the grey light before dawn, the silence of this 'hell of the living' was broken by the shriek of bolts being drawn back in the corridors leading to his cell. Then he heard the voice of the jailer asking what he would like to eat, what furniture he needed, 'For,' said the jailer, 'if you flatter yourself that you are only here for a night, you are very much mistaken.' Everything could be had for a price, the man explained, except books, paper, pens and razors, which were forbidden. For his part, Casanova asked the jailer – a gossipy braggart called Lorenzo – to thank the Lord High Secretary for placing him in a cell on his own, and not in the company of the scoundrels who no doubt infested the other cells. 'What, sir! scoundrels?' Lorenzo expostulated. 'Not at all, not at all. They are only respectable people here, who, for reasons known to their excellencies alone, have to be sequestered from society.' He went on to explain that solitary confinement was an additional punishment.

'The loneliness behind the prison bars is terrible, but it must be learnt by experience to be understood, and such an experience I would not wish even to my enemies.'

Giacomo Casanova, *The Story of My Life*

It was not long before Casanova saw the truth of this, how wretched and mind-numbingly dull it is to be thrown back on one's own resources in a dark cell in which one cannot even stand up straight. A prisoner in solitary confinement, he now understood, would rather be in hell, if only for the sake of the company. Casanova had to make do with the scuttling of the rats, the biting of the fleas, and the chimes of the clock of St Marks. He was not even permitted out of his cell to stretch his legs in the garret. But, in addition to clean bedding and some more comfortable furniture, he was allowed two improving books, *Adoration of the Sacred Heart of our Lord Jesus*

'The wise man tells no one of his business, and the business of the Tribunal of Venice is only to judge and to doom. The guilty party is not required to have any share in the matter; he is like a nail, which to be driven into a wall needs only to be struck.'

Giacomo Casanova, *The Story of My Life*

Christ and *The Mystical City of Sister Mary of Jesus of Agrada*. The first was the work of a 'besotted ignoramus', while the second, more interestingly, was the work of a Spanish nun whose 'grotesque, monstrous, and fantastic visions ... were dignified with the name of revelations'. *The Mystical City*, a 'masterpiece of madness', helped to distract Casanova from his present circumstances, but at the same time began to draw him into its febrile imaginings, and he feared his reason was beginning to desert him. At the same time as his brain was tormented by the wild delusions of Sister Mary, his body suffered under the lead roof in the heat of the dog days of summer. His cell became an oven, and, even though he sat naked, pools of sweat gathered at his feet. To these tortures was added constipation, which caused the eruption of agonizing haemorrhoids, a condition from which he was to suffer for the rest of his life.

But the ever-sanguine libertine lived from day to day, persuading himself he would the next day be freed – or, at the very latest, his release would come on the first day of October, when three new Inquisitors took over from those who had confined him. 'I could not believe,' he recalled, 'that my sentence had been pronounced and confirmed, without my being told of it, or of the reasons by which my judges had been actuated.' But as the first day of October dawned after a sleepless night, no word came from on high. After oscillating for some days between rage and despair, Casanova determined to break out of his prison. He was not going to spend the rest of his days rotting in this hell hole.

Black marble, cold iron

Buoyed up by his belief 'that when a man sets himself determinedly to do something, and thinks of naught but his design, he must succeed despite all difficulties in his path', Casanova devised an escape plan. His cell was directly above the meeting-room of the Inquisitors, and he came to the conclusion that the best way out was downward, through the floor of his cell. But he needed a tool.

In due course he was permitted to take a daily walk in the garret outside his cell, where he was able to rummage among the bits of broken furniture, old chests and bric-a-brac that littered the place. His eye was taken in particular by a piece of polished black marble, an inch thick, six inches long, and three broad, which he hid under his clothes and took back to his cell. Security was surprisingly slack: Casanova observed of his jailer, Lorenzo, 'that if the man had been less of a fool he would most certainly have been more of a scoundrel'. On a later occasion, Casanova was able to smuggle in an iron bar 'as thick as my thumb, and about a foot and a half long'. Using the piece of marble as a whetstone and his saliva instead of oil, he was able – after considerable labour and many a blister – to sharpen the bar to a point. This implement he then concealed in his armchair. His plan was to dig a hole through his floor, then lower himself by knotted sheets attached to his bed into the Inquisitors' chamber below. This was unlocked every morning, which would give him the opportunity to make good his escape, using his spike to deal with any sentry who might be posted there.

One difficulty was how to conceal the results of his excavations. His cell was swept every day, and thus his digging would soon come to light. So he asked Lorenzo to stop the daily sweeping, as the dust raised was, he claimed, giving him a dangerous cough. Lorenzo seemed suspicious, and suggested they wet the floor, but Casanova objected that the damp would also make him ill. To make his point about the dust, one night Casanova pricked his thumb and let several drops of blood soak into his handkerchief, which he waved at Lorenzo the following morning, saying he had suffered a frightful coughing fit. A doctor was summoned, who ordered that the sweeping cease. Abashed, Lorenzo promised that it would not happen again. It would not do for his prisoners to die under his care.

Biding his time in the dark, bone-chilling days of winter, Casanova improvised a lamp out of a porringer filled with salad oil. Twists of cotton from his counterpane served as wicks, and he tricked some flints out of Lorenzo to get a flame. Thus he was able to read the books he was now permitted, thanks to his patron, Senator Bragadin, who had put in a word on his behalf with the Inquisitors. But the lamp had to be concealed when another prisoner came to share his cell for some weeks, and this also held up the commencement of his excavations. When the other prisoner was moved a fortnight after Easter, he at once set to work on the wooden floor, using the lamp to see what he was doing. Once he had broken through the first floorboard, which was some two inches thick, he found another underneath it. When he had broken through that, he found a third below. In all, it took him three weeks to break through the wooden layers, concealing the broken splinters in a napkin. Beneath the boards was another layer, consisting of *terrazzo*, chips of marble set in cement. He found his iron bar made little impact on this substance, but then he recalled Livy's account of Hannibal's soldiers breaking through a rocky obstacle while crossing the Alps by first softening the rocks with vinegar. The next morning he put this theory to the test, although he was not sure whether his resulting success was attributable to the vinegar or to the fact that he was refreshed after a good night's sleep. Underneath the terrazzo lay another floorboard, but Casanova guessed this would be the last obstacle – although difficult to work

'I should have still persisted if my escape had meant death to the whole body of Venetian guards, and even to the Inquisitors themselves. Can the love of country, all holy though it be, prevail in the heart of the man whose country is oppressing him?'

Giacomo Casanova, *The Story of My Life*

on, as it was some ten inches down the hole he had spent so long making. At last, on 24 August, he broke through, and looked down a small aperture into the Inquisitors' room. Unfortunately, he could also see that a beam eight inches thick barred part of his exit, and he was obliged to increase the width of his hole. Eventually he completed his work, making another small aperture to check that his way would be clear. He then stopped up these two chinks, so that the light from his lamp would not betray him.

Hope dashed and rekindled

The following day Lorenzo appeared at the grille and announced that he had good news for his prisoner. Casanova was to be moved, by order of the Court, to a larger cell, where he could stand upright and gaze through two windows across Venice. His hopes of escape dashed, Casanova begged to be left where he was, but realized it would be foolish to argue. At least his furniture would come with him, including the armchair concealing his iron spike. If only, he thought to himself, he could have also taken with him that 'object of so much wasted trouble and hope', his hole. Morosely he followed Lorenzo out of the garret and along a number of passages until he came to his new cell. Although from it he could see as far as the Lido, at that trying moment he did not care much for the view – although in time he came to appreciate the sweet breeze that sighed through the windows, tempering the insufferable heat.

Within two hours of Casanova's arrival at his new abode, Lorenzo reappeared in a rage, foaming at the mouth and blaspheming. He had discovered the hole, and demanded where Casanova had obtained the tools to make it. The guards conducted a search, but found nothing, having failed to turn the armchair over. With typical sang-froid, Casanova declared that if pressed he would say he had obtained the tools from Lorenzo himself, and had returned them to him. At this, the jailer realized that he could be in deep trouble if the authorities believed his security was so slack, and stormed out 'like one possessed'. For a few days, Casanova was made to survive on shrivelled salad, stale bread and putrid meat. A guard made a daily inspection of his cell, sounding out the walls and floor with an iron bar to check for hidden excavations. Casanova noted that he did not check the ceiling.

Once his rage had subsided, Lorenzo, knowing he had been compromised, sought to curry favour with his prisoner, to which end he arranged for Casanova to exchange books with another prisoner, a renegade priest called Balbi. Correspondence was forbidden, as indeed were the means to conduct it, in the form of pens, ink and paper, but Casanova got round this by sharpening the long fingernail of his little finger, which he had used as an earpick. He then dipped this long, sharp nail in the juice of some mulberries, and with it wrote messages at the back of the books he sent to the priest. Via these messages he discovered that Balbi was a fellow libertine, who had been jailed for enjoying 'the good graces of three girls', each of whom had borne him a child. 'In society I should have had nothing more to do with a man of his character,' Casanova observed, with just a whiff of hypocrisy, 'but under the Leads I was obliged to put everything to some use.'

In due course Casanova persuaded Balbi to join him in an escape plan. Knowing that he himself was subject to close scrutiny, Casanova managed to smuggle his iron bar to his co-conspirator. He hid the implement in a folio Bible, which he had specially purchased, ostensibly as a gift for Balbi, but found two inches of the bar were still visible. So he then asked Lorenzo for the largest dish he had, so that, in celebration of St Michael's Day, he could prepare some pasta for the priest who had lent him his books. The bar within the Bible was thus delivered to Balbi, under a huge plate of steaming macaroni swimming in butter – a touch calculated by Casanova to distract Lorenzo, who was so busy trying to prevent the molten butter spilling onto the Bible that he did not notice the protruding ends of the spike.

Once the tool was safely delivered, Balbi quickly set to work. The plan was that the priest would plaster holy pictures all over his walls and ceiling, to conceal the hole he was making in the latter. This ruse appears to have aroused no suspicion, and on the 16 October Casanova heard three light taps on his own ceiling, the signal that Balbi had penetrated the attic and arrived above where Casanova sat, patiently translating an ode of Horace. He had told Balbi not to penetrate all the way through until the very last moment, otherwise the hole would give them away. They waited until the beginning of November, when Casanova knew that the Inquisitors spent three days every year on the mainland. Lorenzo took the opportunity of their absence to get drunk, and never appeared in the prison until late in the morning.

Casanova's plans were complicated by the arrival in his cell of another prisoner, a thin, ugly man called Soradici, a professional informer who was being detained under the suspicion of bearing false witness. But Casanova managed to play on the man's treacherous nature and his inherent gullibility, giving him certain letters to deliver that he knew would end up in the hands of the Inquisitors. When Casanova asked the man to let him have one of the letters back to add a note, he was forced to confess his treachery. Casanova now had him in his power. He claimed that he had been visited in a dream by the Virgin Mary, who

> 'I was fain to escape from this hell on earth, where I was imprisoned by a most detestable tyranny, and I thought only of forwarding this end, with the resolve to succeed, or at all events not to stop before I came to a difficulty which was insurmountable.'
>
> Giacomo Casanova, *The Story of My Life*

> 'The greatest relief of a man in the midst of misfortune is the hope of escaping from it. He sighs for the hour when his sorrows are to end; he thinks he can hasten it by his prayers; he will do anything to know when his torments shall cease.'
>
> Giacomo Casanova, *The Story of My Life*

ABOVE Casanova as a young man, after a portrait by the Venetian painter Pietro Longhi.

had asked him to forgive Soradici, so that the curse that the latter had drawn on himself could be lifted. Furthermore, at an appointed time, she would send down one of her angels disguised as a man to break open the roof of the prison – as long as Soradici renounced his business of spying.

On 31 October the appointed hour came, as did the angel – in the unprepossessing form of a hirsute Father Balbi, jumping down into Casanova's cell from the roof space. Soradici was commanded to cut off the angel's beard, and also that of his cell mate – for bearded men on the loose in Venice could only be escapees from the state's prisons, where razors were forbidden. Casanova hoisted himself up through the hole in the ceiling to reconnoitre the way out. Returning, he spent some hours cutting up sheets, coverlets and bedding to make ropes. 'I took care to make the knots myself and to be assured of their strength,' he recalled, 'for a single weak knot might cost us our lives.' He had found that the wooden roof struts were half rotten, and when Balbi and he climbed back into the roof space they made short work of this barrier. All that remained were the leaden sheets of the roof itself:

> I could not do it by myself, because it was riveted. The monk [Balbi] came to my aid, and by dint of driving the bar between the gutter and the lead I succeeded in loosening it, and then, heaving at it with our shoulders, we beat it up till the opening was wide enough.

But when he poked his head out into the free air of Venice, he was distressed to see that the moon shone so brightly that he and his companion would cast great shadows below and give themselves away. They were obliged to wait until the moon set at eleven o'clock.

When darkness returned, they crawled up the smooth lead plates of the roof, fearful that every move might cause a slip and send them into the black abyss below. Once astride the roof, Casanova searched in vain for a way down. But he was not a man to despair, and, making his way along the ridge he spotted below him a dormer window. There followed some remarkable acrobatics involving the rope of knotted sheets and a fortuitously discovered ladder, all conducted at a perilous height above the ground. 'I shudder still when I think of this awful moment,' Casanova recalled, 'which cannot be conceived in all its horror.' Eventually, they got themselves down to the window, and into a room, and from there they made their way through the passages and staircases and chambers of the darkened palace, on one occasion having to use the iron bar to break through the door of the chancery.

Beyond the borders of the Republic

Squeezing through the hole they'd made they suffered many cuts from the splintered wood, and stopped to dress their wounds. They also changed their clothes, to give a semblance of respectability prior to presenting themselves to the outside world. Casanova put on an exquisite hat trimmed with Spanish lace, and adorned with a white feather. 'I must have looked like a man who has been to a dance and has spent the rest of the night in a disorderly house,' he later wrote, 'though the only foil to my reasonable elegance of attire was the bandages round my knees.' At this point he was spotted at the window by someone in the courtyard below, who went to fetch the gate-keeper. The latter fortunately assumed Casanova was a courtier who had been locked inadvertently in the palace overnight, and, confounded by the error he assumed he had made, let them out without uttering a word.

Freedom was theirs, but they must first escape beyond the borders of the Serene Republic. Casanova wept with relief as they took a gondola from the Piazza San Marco across the waters to the mainland. He had loudly instructed the gondoliers to take them to Fusina, so that passers-by could hear, but once safely underway he changed his instruction: they were to head for Mestre. Thus any pursuers would be thrown off the scent. Once on the mainland, Casanova parted company with his despised companion, to whom in his memoirs he constantly attributes the worst qualities – cowardice, stupidity, sullenness, want of energy – refusing to acknowledge that without Balbi he might still have been incarcerated in the Leads.

Casanova made his way northward beyond the territories of Venice, and, in the depth of winter, crossed the Alps. He was not to see his homeland again for another 18 years. Such was his anxiety to put a great distance between himself and his persecutors that in just over a month, having travelled via Augsburg and Strasbourg, he was once more in Paris. It was 5 January, the very day that a religious maniac called Robert-François Damiens tried to kill Louis XV with a knife. Casanova was to witness his hideously brutal public execution, pulled limb from limb by four horses in the Place de Grève. But that is another story – just one of many chapters in the life of this extraordinary man.

> 'The safety I sought was beyond the borders of the Republic, and thitherward I began to bend my steps. Already there in spirit, I must needs be there in body also.'
>
> Giacomo Casanova, *The Story of My Life*

THE UNDERGROUND RAILROAD

The escape network for fugitive slaves, c.1810-65

In the first half of the 19th century, the Northern and Southern states of America became increasingly polarized over the issue of slavery. For some who opposed this inhuman institution as an affront to God and humanity fine words were not enough. Hundreds of activists –freeborn blacks, former slaves and white abolitionists – organized the so-called Underground Railroad, an informal network of clandestine routes and discreet safe houses by which fugitive slaves were helped to reach safety, and liberty, in the North or in Canada.

A great variety of people – including John Brown, Harriet Tubman and Henry David Thoreau – acted as 'conductors', leading runaways ('passengers' or 'cargo') between 'stations' or 'depots', which were looked after by 'stationmasters', while those who donated money or gave food to support the operation were known as 'stockholders'. Considerable ingenuity was required to counter the efforts of the authorities and freelance bounty hunters to recapture fugitives. The original Fugitive Slave Act of 1793 left the responsibility of catching runaways to officials from the states where the slaves had been held. However, the Fugitive Slave Act of 1850, a component of the notorious Compromise of that year between North and South, gave the federal authorities the power to arrest runaways even in non-slave states and return them to their owners. Fugitives were not allowed to testify in their own defence, and

> '**RANAWAY**, a negro woman and two children; a few days before she went off, I burnt her with a hot iron, on the left side of her face, I tried to make the letter M.'

An advertisement placed by Micajah Ricks, a slave owner, in the North Carolina *Raleigh Standard*, 18 July 1839. For decades, the Southern press was full of such advertisements.

were tried without a jury. Under this new dispensation, many free blacks were also unlawfully arrested and sent into slavery in the South, and anyone caught helping a runaway was made liable to a heavy fine and imprisonment.

Despite these vicissitudes, the Underground Railroad continued to operate right up to Emancipation and the end of the Civil War in 1865, and some 500 slaves a year – perhaps a total of as many as 30,000 – obtained their freedom in this way. The stories of many of them were recorded by William Still, a son of freed slaves who was long associated with the Anti-Slavery Office in Philadelphia, and who became the chairman of the Vigilance Committee of the Philadelphia branch of the Underground Railroad. Interviewing one of the fugitives who arrived at his office, he discovered that the man was in fact his own brother, from whom he had been separated in childhood.

OPPOSITE The 'resurrection' of runaway slave Henry 'Box' Brown, who had had himself posted from the slave state of Virginia to Philadelphia and freedom.

The resurrection of Henry 'Box' Brown

One of the most bizarre tales told by Still is that of the slave who posted himself to freedom. This man was Henry Brown, born into slavery in Virginia in 1815, and who in 1830 began work in a tobacco factory in Richmond. It was in 1849 that he devised his escape plan, persuading a sympathetic white storekeeper called Samuel Smith to box him up and dispatch him to Philadelphia, and to alert James M. McKim of the Vigilance Committee in that city of his imminent arrival.

> 'Men of almost every degree of wit called on me in the migrating season. Some who had more wits than they knew what to do with; runaway slaves with plantation manners, who listened from time to time, like the fox in the fable, as if they heard the hounds a-baying on their track ...'

Henry David Thoreau, *Walden* (1854). Thoreau not only helped runaways, he also provided one of the most eloquent voices in the anti-slavery campaign, and defended John Brown's rebellion.

The box, lined with baize, measured 2 feet 8 inches deep, 2 feet wide, and 3 feet long. For sustenance, Brown supplied himself with a bladder of water and a few small biscuits, and to maintain his air supply took with him a large gimlet to make holes in the packing case. 'Satisfied that it would be far better to peril his life for freedom in this way,' Still writes, 'than to remain under the galling yoke of Slavery, he entered his box,' which was then nailed up and fastened with five hickory hoops by his friend, a freedman called James A. Smith. The case was marked 'This side up with care.'

This last injunction was largely ignored by those who handled the box over the 26 hours of its journey, and for some miles Brown found himself upside down. Regardless of these difficulties, the box eventually arrived at its destination, the Anti-Slavery Office in Philadelphia. Ready to receive it were McKim, William Still, and two others. Still recounts what happened next:

All was quiet. The door had been safely locked. The proceedings commenced. Mr McKim rapped quietly on the lid of the box and called out, 'All right!' Instantly came the answer from within, 'All right, sir!'

The witnesses will never forget that moment. Saw and hatchet quickly had the five hickory hoops cut and the lid off, and the marvellous resurrection of Brown ensued. Rising up in his box, he reached out his hand, saying, 'How do you do, gentlemen?' The little assemblage hardly knew what to think or do at the moment. He was about as wet as if he had come up out of the Delaware. Very soon he remarked that, before leaving Richmond he had selected for his arrival-hymn (if he lived) the Psalm beginning with these words: *'I waited patiently for the Lord, and He heard my prayer.'* And most touchingly did he sing the psalm, much to his own relief, as well as to the delight of his small audience.

Subsequently Brown became a prominent speaker on behalf of the Anti-Slavery Society, touring with a panorama entitled *The Mirror of Slavery*, initially in the North, and subsequently in Great Britain, whither he was obliged to go following the

> Rising up in his box, he reached out his hand, saying, "How do you do, gentlemen?"
>
> Henry 'Box' Brown greets the free air of Philadelphia

passage of the Fugitive Slave Act. He did not return to the USA until 1875, by which time he had built up a career as a showman, performing as a mesmerist and a magician under the name Professor H. Box Brown. One of the men who aided his escape, Samuel Smith, was not so fortunate: when he tried to post two more runaways north they were caught and he was imprisoned for eight years. 'Though he lost all his property,' the *New York Tribune* reported on his release in 1856,

> ... though he was refused witnesses on his trial ... though for five long months, in hot weather, he was kept heavily chained in a cell four by eight feet in dimensions; though he received five dreadful stabs, aimed at his heart, by a bribed assassin, nevertheless he still rejoices in the motives which prompted him to 'undo the heavy burdens, and let the oppressed go free'.

The battle of the barn

There is a passage in Byron's *Childe Harold's Pilgrimage* that inspired many slaves to liberate themselves:

> Hereditary bondsmen! know ye not
> Who would be free themselves must strike the blow.

It is quoted by William Still (as 'He who would be free, himself must strike the blow') in relation to the case of Robert Jackson, alias Wesley Harris, a 22-year-old runaway who arrived in Philadelphia in 1853. His former owner, a Mrs Carroll of Harper's Ferry, Virginia, was a kind woman, he said, and promised her slaves their freedom on her death, but in the meantime hired them out to settle her late husband's debts. Her manager, however, was a cruel man, and when he had attempted to flog Harris for 'some trifling cause', Harris had resisted, and, turning the tables, had given the manager himself a beating. Following this incident he was told he was to be sold, and this hardened in him a determination to escape.

> I told them if they took me they would have to take me dead or crippled.
>
> Wesley Harris defies his would-be captors

At midnight one Saturday he duly made a break for the North, accompanied by his friend Craven Matterson and Matterson's two brothers. After two days they found themselves in Terrytown, Maryland, where, Harris later told Still, 'we were informed by a friendly coloured man of the danger we were in and of the bad character of the place towards coloured people, especially those who were escaping to freedom'. They hid in the

‘I then drew a sword I had brought with me, and was about cutting my way to the door when I was shot by one of the men ...’

Wesley Harris makes his break for freedom

woods, and then in a thicket near a barn, but their hiding place was exposed by a dog, whose barking alerted his master, the farmer. They told the farmer they were merely journeying to Gettysburg, in the free state of Pennsylvania, to visit some relatives. The farmer said he knew they were runaways. 'He then offered friendly advice, talked like a Quaker, and urged us to go with him to his barn for protection. After much persuasion, we consented to go with him.'

Arriving at the barn, the farmer and his daughter provided them with breakfast, which cheered their spirits. The farmer told them to hide in the straw till nightfall, when he would show them the road to Gettysburg. They fell asleep, but at noon were awakened by the sound of men's voices outside. Then eight armed men with ropes entered the barn, asking the owner if he had any long straw, to which he replied that he had, and then, coming across the fugitives as if by chance, they, in feigned surprise, asked the owner if he harboured runaway slaves in his barn. He answered, 'No,' and pretended to be entirely ignorant of their being in his barn. Despite this

I NEVER LOST A PASSENGER

Harriet Tubman, one of the most famous conductors on the Underground Railroad, was born a slave sometime around the year 1821. With the aid of Quakers in her native Maryland, she made her bid for freedom in 1849, telling a friend as she left that she was 'bound for the promised land'. The story of Moses leading the Israelites out of slavery in Egypt to the promised land was an inspiration to many runaways, as reflected in the Negro spiritual 'Go Down Moses':

> When Israel was in Egypt's land,
> Let my people go;
> Oppressed so hard they could not stand,
> Let my people go.

When Tubman herself became a conductor on the Underground Railroad she did so with such success – over eight years she made 19 covert sorties into Maryland, bringing more than 300 slaves to freedom – that she herself became known as 'Moses'. It was something of which she was justifiably proud, particularly as Southern slave owners had posted a bounty of $40,000 for her capture: 'I can say what most conductors can't say – I never ran my train off the track and I never lost a passenger.' During the Civil War she served with Union forces as a laundress, nurse and spy, and subsequently agitated for women's suffrage. She was not granted a pension for her Civil War work until three decades after the end of the conflict, and died in poverty in 1913.

attempt at deception, Harris knew
they had been betrayed. The
armed men demanded to see the
fugitives' passes, and when they
could produce none, informed
them they would be brought
before a magistrate. 'I told them,'
Harris relates, 'if they took me
they would have to take me dead
or crippled.' At this point one of
his friends shot and badly
wounded the treacherous farmer –
their would-be apprehenders did
not realize that the runaways were
themselves armed – and Harris
himself aimed a shot at the
constable, but the latter raised an
arm which deflected Harris's aim
as he fired. Harris continues:

> I again fired on the pursuers,
> but do not know whether I hit
> anybody or not. I then drew a
> sword I had brought with me,
> and was about cutting my way
> to the door when I was shot by
> one of the men, receiving the
> entire contents of one load of a
> double-barrelled gun in my left
> arm, that being the arm with

ABOVE Harriet Tubman, one of the most successful conductors on
the Underground Railroad. 'I never ran my train off the track,' she
boasted, 'and I never lost a passenger.'

> which I was defending myself. The load brought me to the ground, and I was
> unable to make further struggle for myself. I was then badly beaten with guns,
> &c. In the meantime, my friend Craven, who was defending himself, was shot
> badly in the face, and most violently beaten until he was conquered and tied.
> The two young brothers of Craven stood still, without making the least
> resistance.

Thus they found themselves once more in captivity. Harris was bleeding so badly
from his wound that he was kept a prisoner in a tavern in Terrytown, and not taken
further. Here his wounds were dressed and 32 pieces of shot extracted from his arm.
For three days he was delirious and thought likely to die, and even after some
weeks, though greatly recovered, he was still very weak. Harris was visited by the

tavern's black cook, Mrs Smith, and a man called James Matthews, who procured for him a rope, and also four nails. This, and the help of more sympathizers, was all he needed to make good his escape:

> On Friday night, October 14th, I fastened my nails in under the window sill, tied my rope to the nails, threw my shoes out of the window, put the rope in my mouth, then took hold of it with my well hand, clambered into the window, very weak, but I managed to let myself down to the ground. I was so weak, that I could scarcely walk, but I managed to hobble off to a place three-quarters of a mile from the tavern, where a friend had fixed upon for me to go ...

'O, old master don't cry for me,
For I am going to Canada
Where coloured men are free.'

Anon. parody of the song 'O, Susanna', quoted by John W. Jones, an Underground Railroad agent, in a letter to William Still, 6 June 1860

Here, the following night, he was furnished with a swift horse and was taken by an unnamed black conductor via an indirect route to Gettysburg. From Gettysburg he made his way to Still and his colleagues in Philadelphia, and from thence he proceeded to Canada, where he became a naturalized citizen and found work as a brakesman on the Great Western Railroad. The three Matterson brothers were not so lucky: sent to Baltimore, they were sold for $1,200 each.

****

It was to be a long struggle for freedom – including four years of bitter civil war – but the stories from the Underground Railroad continued to serve as an inspiration, as William Still observes in the preface to his book:

> While the grand little army of abolitionists was waging its untiring warfare for freedom, prior to the rebellion, no agency encouraged them like the heroism of fugitives. The pulse of the four millions of slaves and their desire for freedom, were better felt through 'The Underground Railroad', than through any other channel.

OVER THE ICY PASSES

William Brydon, the sole European to survive the British retreat from Kabul, 1842

For days Captain Backhouse and his fellow officers had peered westward from the grey walls of Jalalabad, looking out for a distant cloud of dust. Before them the river meandered across a dun plain dotted with orchards of almond and apricot; it was still winter, and the trees were bare and gaunt. Beyond the plain rose the snow-covered mountains, and far away across the mountains lay Kabul. Then, just after midday on 13 January 1842, someone spotted a lone horseman approaching the walls of the city. The rider was slumped in his saddle, and those watching his slow progress could see a dark stain spreading out from beneath his hat. As the man dismounted it was clear he was badly wounded. In a hoarse voice, his blood-caked lips barely moving, he introduced himself: Assistant Surgeon Brydon, 5th Native Infantry, Bengal Army. His horse, freed from its burden, fell to the ground, dead with exhaustion.

Dr Brydon had been expected – but not alone. With him there should have been an army of 4,500 men, together with 12,000 camp followers – the entire garrison of Kabul. In the expectation that they would not be long in coming, the soldiers on the walls of Jalalabad lit beacon fires to guide the stragglers to safety. Hours passed, and then days, but only a handful of survivors – all Indian sepoy troops – came down from the icy passes to the west. Not for the last time, the Afghanis had shown that it was one thing to invade their country, another thing altogether to try to tame it.

The Great Game

After the defeat of Napoleon in 1815, the Russian Bear began to replace Boney as Britain's number-one bogeyman. In particular the British feared that Russia's expansion into Central Asia threatened India, the jewel in Britain's colonial crown. Between India and the steppes of Central Asia lay the mountainous kingdom of Afghanistan, and the British calculated that if they could maintain Afghanistan as a buffer state, they could keep the Russian Bear at bay. To this end, in 1839 the East India Company, the administrators of British India, sent an army over the Khyber Pass to Kabul to depose the uncooperative Amir Dost Mohammed Khan, and replace him with a former ruler, Shah Shuja.

PREVIOUS PAGE The arrival of William Brydon at the walls of Jalalabad, after Lady Butler's celebrated painting *Remnants of an Army*.

That was the easy part. After Dost Mohammed had been driven into hiding, a garrison of 4,500 men – mostly Indian sepoys commanded by British officers – was established in Kabul, under General Sir Willoughby Cotton, and another in Kandahar under General William Nott. With peace apparently restored, the wives and families of British officers, and even of sepoys, joined their menfolk in Kabul. This sent entirely the wrong message: the Afghans believed that the British had come to stay, and began to think of how they could get rid of them.

The invaders had built their cantonment in a vulnerable position, on low marshland surrounded by hills. On the hills were forts, and in the forts were Afghans. What was worse, the British had placed their food stores outside the walls of the cantonment. But they remained complacent: when Cotton was replaced by Major General William Elphinstone in 1841, he informed his successor that he would have nothing to do. 'All is peace,' he said.

> Yesterday it had been impossible to write the horrible news of the day, and my soul is now filled with anguish at the melancholy catastrophe which has overtaken the Cabool Force – all are lost – the force is annihilated to a man.
>
> Captain Julius Brockman Backhouse of the Jalalabad garrison, in his diary, 14 January 1842

From bad to worse

Elphinstone was a poor choice – he had even said so himself – but Lord Auckland, the governor general of India who had initiated the Afghan War, had insisted he go. The elderly major general had not seen action since Waterloo, and suffered so badly from gout and rheumatism that he had to be carried everywhere in a litter. He also suffered from flatulence and incontinence, and his mind was becoming increasingly confused. This might not have mattered had all indeed been peace, as Cotton had averred – but it was not. Shah Shuja's inept government became more and more unpopular, and attacks on British soldiers were increasing – they were even sniped on while they went about their business within the cantonment. Things came to a head on 2 November 1841 when an angry mob broke into the British residency and murdered Sir Alexander Burnes, the deputy British envoy, together with his younger brother and another officer.

Elphinstone, declining further into senility, was paralysed into inaction. The British envoy, Sir William Macnaghten, sent a message to General Sale in Jalalabad, asking him to take over the Kabul command, but the Afghans had cut the route between the two cities. In desperation, Macnaghten decided to try parleying with Akbar Khan, the son of the ousted Dost Mohammed. On 23 December he agreed to meet Akbar Khan

> You will have nothing to do here. All is peace.
>
> General Sir Willoughby Cotton, to Major General William Elphinstone, who in 1841 succeeded him as commander in Kabul

accompanied by only three officers. When they reached the appointed place, the Britons were immediately seized, and Akbar Khan himself shot Macnaghten with the pistol the British envoy had given him only the day before. The bodies of the four men were hacked to pieces and their heads and limbs paraded through the streets of Kabul. Elphinstone at last got the point. Assured by the Afghans of a safe passage, he ordered his army to march back to India.

The retreat

It was midwinter, there were many passes to cross, and the Afghan tribesmen along the route were to prove far from friendly. William Brydon was just one of the 16,500 men, women and children who left the Kabul cantonment around nine in the morning on 6 January 1842. As part of the agreement with the Afghans, the British were obliged to leave behind nearly all of their artillery, together with a number of officers and their families as hostages. Snow had been falling steadily for three weeks.

> 'If only the army had been commanded by the memsahibs all might have been well.'
>
> Sita Ram, From *Sepoy to Subedar* (1873). A sepoy in the Bengal Army, Sita Ram was taken prisoner by the Afghans in the retreat from Kabul.

The attacks began almost immediately, the rearguard being fired on from the ramparts of Kabul itself. The column made no more than five miles that first day, and was obliged to spend the night in the open, without shelter. Hundreds died of cold. Further on, at Bootkhak, Akbar Khan appeared, demanding more hostages in return for safe conduct. Once more he failed to keep his word, and as the column entered the five-mile defile of the Khoord Kabul Pass, they were subjected to continuous fire from the heights on either side. Despite gallant rearguard actions by the 44th Regiment of Foot, some 3,000 dead or dying were left behind that day.

More passes, and more ambushes, were to follow. Many of the soldiers had such badly frostbitten fingers that they could not pull the triggers of their muskets. On 11 January Akbar Khan demanded that Elphinstone, together with his second-in-command, Brigadier Shelton, should hand themselves over as hostages. Elphinstone agreed, abnegating all responsibility as a commander. The next day the column arrived at the crest of the Jigdalak Pass, only to find it blocked by barricades of thorn brush, while thousands of tribesmen attacked their rear, cutting up great numbers. 'The confusion now was terrible,' Brydon recalled, 'all discipline was at an end.' Few managed to pass this obstacle alive.

The last stand took place on the morning of 13 January at Gandamak. Forty-five officers and men, mostly of the 44th Foot but also including Dr Brydon, found themselves

> 'So terrible had been the effects of the cold and exposure upon the Native Troops that they were unable to resist the attacks of the Enemy.'
>
> From William Brydon's own account, given to General Sale after his arrival in Jalalabad

ABOVE William Barnes Wollen's painting of the last stand of the 44th Foot at Gandamak, 13 January 1842.

surrounded on a low hill. The Afghans circling them tried to persuade them that they would come to no harm, but then came the snipers' bullets, and then the pack closed in. It was a massacre from which only six officers, including Brydon, escaped, riding hell for leather for Jalalabad. They got as far as Fatehabad, only four miles from the city, where they were set upon once more, and five of the officers killed. Brydon was wounded in the knee and the left hand, and an Afghan sword sliced off part of his skull. He was only saved from having his brains spattered across the road by a copy of *Blackwood's Magazine*, which he had stuffed under his forage cap to keep out the cold. Quite why he was allowed to continue to Jalalabad is unclear. Perhaps the Afghans intended to leave one man alive as a warning.

Aftermath

Brydon's adventures were not yet over. Jalalabad was cut off from British India by tribesmen holding the Khyber Pass to the east. An earthquake in February virtually destroyed the city's defences, and shortly afterwards Akbar Khan arrived at the gates. His assaults were repulsed, and on 7 April the 'illustrious garrison' counterattacked, forcing Akbar Khan to retreat back to Kabul. On 16 April a relief force from India forced the Khyber Pass and reached Jalalabad,

When you're wounded and
  left on Afghanistan's plains
And the women come out to
  cut up what remains
Just roll to your rifle and
  blow out your brains
An' go to your Gawd like a
  soldier.

Rudyard Kipling, 'The Young British Soldier' (1892)

where a scratch band greeted them with the old Jacobite tune 'Oh, but ye've been lang o' coming'.

In the autumn of 1842 the British assembled an 'Army of Retribution' and marched on Kabul, where they rescued a handful of British prisoners and burnt down the citadel and the Great Bazaar. Shah Shuja, deserted by his British sponsors, had been assassinated in April, and the *status ante bellum* was restored. The whole misguided adventure of the First Afghan War became known as 'Auckland's Folly', after the governor general whose idea it had been. As subsequent events have illustrated, it is easier to go into Afghanistan than it is to get out.

Brydon himself – who became famed as 'the Last Man' – returned to India, married the daughter of an East India merchant, fathered eight children, and was promoted to surgeon, serving with the 40th Native Infantry in Burma. During the Indian Mutiny of 1857 he found himself besieged in Lucknow, where he had another lucky escape when a bullet penetrated his lower spine, but failed to kill him. Two years later he retired from the Indian service and set up home in Easter Ross in the north of Scotland. He died, peacefully, in 1873.

DELIVERANCE FROM RAT HELL

The mass breakout of Union officers from Libby Prison, Richmond, Virginia, 1864

Before the advent of the Geneva Convention, conditions for prisoners of war were often grim. Nowhere was this more true than in Confederate prisons during the American Civil War, where the mortality rate among Union officers and men was appallingly high – nearly one-third in the case of the notorious Andersonville Prison in Georgia. Escape, therefore, was not just a patriotic duty; it could also be a matter of personal survival. No doubt both thoughts were in the minds of the men involved in one of the most successful mass escapes of the war. This took place in February 1864, when over a hundred Union officers escaped from Libby Prison in Richmond, Virginia. More than half of them made it back to Union lines.

Prior to the war Libby Prison, a three-storey brick building on Tobacco Road, had been the home of a ship's chandlery and grocery business run by Captain Luther Libby and his son George. With the outbreak of war, and the urgent need of somewhere to house Union prisoners, Captain Libby was given 48 hours to vacate his premises – but the sign reading 'L. Libby & Son, Ship Chandlers' on the northwest corner was never removed, and the name stuck.

Filth and monotony

Prison conditions in the South were not only squalid, but also desperately overcrowded – as attested by John Bray of the 1st New Jersey Cavalry, who was captured in November 1863. At first Bray was held in another building in Richmond, the Pemberton Factory Prison. Here 1,120 prisoners were held in four floors, each measuring 25 by 100 feet – giving less than 9 square feet per prisoner. In an article in the April 1864 edition of *Harper's New Monthly Magazine* Bray described the conditions he met when he first entered the prison:

> The building was filthy to the last degree; there was not a clean spot anywhere; the hold of a slave-ship could not have been more offensive. The mere appearance of the place was sufficient to sicken sensitive stomachs. Some of the prisoners who had been exhausted by their long journey did actually faint upon entering their quarters.

Once they became inured to the squalor, prisoners faced an unremitting cycle of soulless monotony:

PREVIOUS PAGE The Libby Prison for Union officers in Richmond, Virginia, witnessed one of the most dramatic escapes of the Civil War.

ABOVE The infamous prisoner-of-war camp at Andersonville, Georgia, where the appalling conditions led to the deaths of nearly one-third of the Union soldiers held there.

> Of course there was little amusement in sitting, day after day, on the floor of our prison and looking into one another's faces like so many gaping imbeciles. Isolated from the world, hardly permitted to look from our small windows into the streets without, we could only find within ourselves the diversion we needed, and our thought was far too monotonous to suggest any variety of entertainment.

The only pastime was 'skirmishing', which entailed thoroughly shaking each other to get rid of 'vermin' – presumably lice and fleas. Without this vigorous action, 'many of us would have been inevitably overcome, and probably carried out piecemeal at the keyholes, or dragged bodily to the dens of the persecutors'. The food was of a quality higher than might have been expected, Bray said, but inadequate in quantity: the daily allowance was 'half a loaf of bread ... a piece of fresh meat about two inches square, and a pint of bean soup, all without salt'.

After some minor misdemeanour, Bray was removed to Libby Prison for punishment. This consisted of 'bucking and gagging' – a process 'by no means calculated to inspire one with admiration for rebel tenderness or humanity', involving as it did tying the victim's hands together at the wrists, then drawing the arms over the knees, where they were pinioned. The victim was then gagged, and left on the floor in this condition for eight hours. It was not only uncomfortable, but also deeply humiliating.

One man's home run

Prisoners could augment their rations by bartering with the guards. Some exchanged their cavalry boots or other items for better rations; Bray had managed to swap his smart Union uniform for the tattered grey jacket and trousers belonging to the Confederate officer in charge of his floor at Pemberton. In this guise, on 10 January 1864, after his transfer to Libby, he slipped past the guards and out of the prison, without once being challenged. But there were still many miles of enemy territory between himself and freedom, and it was the middle of winter.

> Of course the utmost vigilance was necessary as the whole Peninsula was full of pickets, mostly mounted, and while, therefore, pressing forward with all the rapidity possible, under the circumstances, I kept my eyes on constant duty, scanning closely every marsh and thicket lest some enemy should unexpectedly appear and arrest my flight.

The first night, without blanket or overcoat, he dropped exhausted in the snow in a swamp, and fell asleep. He only just survived freezing to death, but the next morning struggled to his feet and continued on his journey. On his way he encountered a negro, who was not fooled by his Confederate uniform:

> 'Yer can't come dat game on dis chil',' he said, with a sparkle in his eye; 'I knows yer, Sar; you'se a Yankee pris'ner 'scaped from Richmon'.' Then, as if to reassure me, he hurriedly added, 'But, Lor' bless yer, massa, I won't tell on yer; I'se real glad yer's got away.'

The man led him to some friends of his, a negro couple, who gave him food before he continued his journey.

Every now and again Bray had to dart off the road at the sight of pickets and scouts in the distance. Once he was too late, and a pistol ball whistled past him as he dived into the undergrowth. Thereafter he kept off the beaten track, wading through swamps and streams and thickets. At one point brittle twigs breaking beneath his feet alerted some nearby rebel soldiers, and for an hour or more he had to lie still as they searched the area. Eventually, on the evening of 12 January, he reached what he hoped were

'My Dear Wife. – Yours received – no hopes of exchange – send corn starch – want socks – no money – rheumatism in left shoulder – pickles very good – send sausages – God bless you – kiss the baby – Hail Columbia! – Your devoted husband.'

An inmate's letter sent from Libby Prison, printed in the *Christian Recorder*, 11 February 1865. Prisoners were limited to six lines per letter.

the Union lines at Williamsburg, although he was not sure that he was not lost, perhaps still in Confederate territory. Suddenly, in the dark, he felt a heavy hand grasp his shoulder while a loud voice exclaimed, 'Hello, here! – who is this? A spy?' He started, he said, as if he'd been hit by a musket ball, but, trusting in his instinct that he had indeed reached safety, he declared: 'I'm a Union soldier escaped from Richmond.' All suspicion was cast aside, and he was greeted with open arms and cheered as the hero of the hour. Bray's reward was two weeks furlough.

> I think I would not have had a comrade see me as I lay on the floor of Libby, knotted into the most grotesque sort of tangle – rolled up, as it were, into a little heap – for a whole year's pay and all the medals I may ever win.

John Bray, 1st New Jersey Cavalry, on his experience of being 'bucked and gagged' in Libby Prison

Mass breakout

The mass breakout from Libby a month later was a much more organized affair, under the overall command of Colonel Thomas E. Rose, who had been wounded and captured at the Battle of Chickamauga the previous September. The plan was to dig a tunnel, starting in a dank, dark, abandoned part of the prison known, after its teeming denizens, as 'Rat Hell'. The would-be escapers accessed this unpleasant place down a chimney, and the two feet of straw on the floor proved useful cover both for those involved in excavating the tunnel – three teams of five men – and for the earth that they dug out. A further advantage was that the place was so vile that the guards only gave it the most cursory of inspections. One of the leading Union officers involved, Major A.G. Hamilton, remarked on the 'unpleasant feature of having to hear hundreds of rats squeal all the time, while they ran over the diggers almost without a sign of fear'.

After 17 days of excavation, the tunnellers surfaced – as planned – inside a shed within the yard of a nearby warehouse. On breaking through, Colonel Rose announced to his men that 'The Underground Railroad to God's Country is open!' On the night of 9 February, a total of 109 Union officers, in groups of two or three, crawled along the tunnel and gathered in the shed, before casually walking out of the warehouse yard. They were far enough away from the prison to be unnoticed by the guards, and no one else seemed too concerned – indeed, no one in Richmond had conceived that the Yankee prisoners could be capable of such an audacious escapade. The last men left long before daybreak, and it was not until morning

> No tongue can tell ... how the poor fellow[s] passed among the squealing rats, – enduring the sickening air, the deathly chill, the horrible interminable darkness.

Lieutenant Charles H. Moran, one of the escapers who was recaptured, on the experience of tunnelling out of 'Rat Hell'

> ❝ I ... started due north, taking the North Star for my guide. ❞

Captain I.N. Johnston, *Four Months in Libby* (1893)

roll call that the guards realized they were over a hundred men short. They could not believe that so many men could have disappeared overnight, and assumed the Yankees were up to their old tricks, swapping places at roll call and getting themselves counted twice or thrice, or hiding round corners – something they seemed to find amusing.

But after several recounts, the awful truth dawned. By this time the escapers had had a 12-hour head start. Without maps or compasses, they used the North Star to guide them to safety – just as the fugitive slaves on the Underground Railroad had done. Out of the 109 men who escaped, two were drowned in the James River, 48 (including Colonel Rose) were recaptured, but 59 succeeded in making it to the Union lines.

The breakout was a boost to the morale of the remaining prisoners. There was considerable hilarity when a roll call was ordered in the middle of the night after a sentry saw something down a sewer. It turned out to be his own shadow. After this the prisoners joked that when the warden, Major Thomas P. Turner, came to inspect their rooms he pressed his knees tightly together in case one of them slipped like a mischievous piglet between his legs.

The breakout was also something of a propaganda coup for the North, and in his article in *Harper's Monthly* John Bray expressed the hopes of many who had escaped from Libby:

> ... someday I hope to ride into [Richmond] with my comrades of the New Jersey First, with the old flag streaming over us – expelling before us as we go the miserable traitors whose hands would drag that flag, if they could, in the dust, and put out forever the lustrous promise shining on its folds. When we march into Richmond I trust that there will be with us men of darker hue than ours, who, having fought their way from a prison-house worse than the Libby, will have won the right to rejoice in the triumph of the Stars and Stripes.

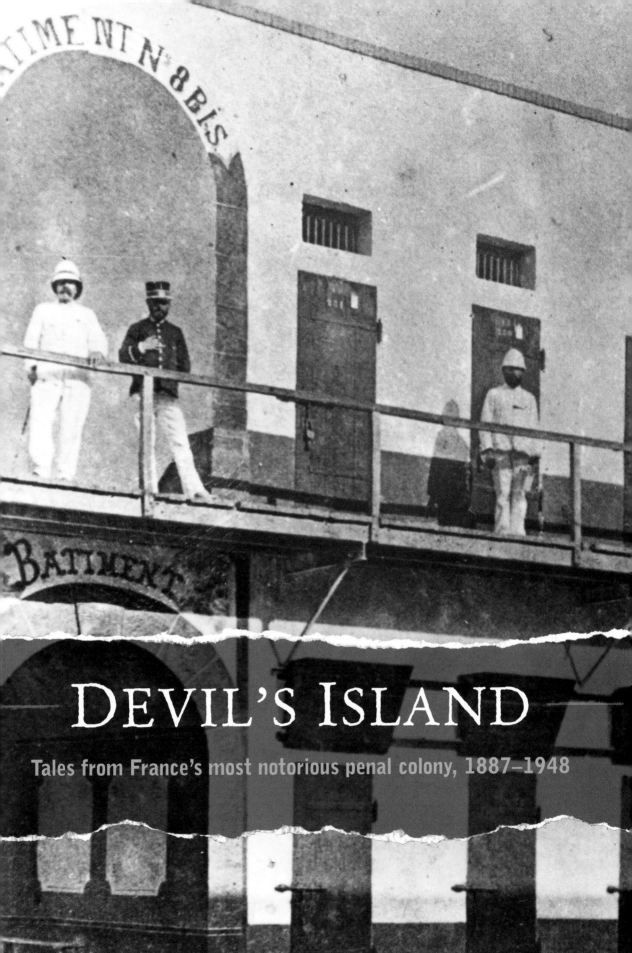

DEVIL'S ISLAND

Tales from France's most notorious penal colony, 1887–1948

Some ten miles off the coast of French Guiana and the mouth of the Kirou River lie the Îles de Salut, three rocky, sweltering, disease-infested islets on which, in 1852, the Emperor Napoleon III established a notorious penal colony. The first convicts to be sent there were opponents of Napoleon's coup d'état, but soon they were joined by common criminals, from brutal killers to petty thieves. The French referred to the convict settlement on the Îles de Salut, the Islands of Salvation, as *le bagne de Cayenne* – a *bagne* being a penal colony and Cayenne the capital of French Guiana, France's only colony in South America. Because so few ever returned alive, the convicts themselves referred to the colony as *la guillotine sèche*, the dry guillotine.

The smallest and northernmost islet, just three-quarters of a mile long by quarter of a mile wide, was initially a refuge for the colony's lepers, but later, because it was so remote, it was designated a high-security area for those convicted of treason or espionage, political undesirables and the most vicious criminals. Here among the palm trees and the barren rocks they were condemned to years of brutalization, hard labour, exhaustion, dysentery, malaria and yellow fever. Thousands succumbed, but rather than giving them proper burial, the guards would throw their corpses into the sea for the sharks to eat. Few would argue with the name of this awful place: Île de Diable – Devil's Island.

An anarchist wins his freedom

Few men succeeded in escaping from *le bagne*, and if they did, even fewer avoided recapture. Clément Duval, who was sentenced to hard labour on Devil's Island in 1887, tried to escape over 20 times, but it was not until 1901 that he was finally successful.

Duval had served in the infantry during the Franco-Prussian War, during which he contracted smallpox and was badly wounded by a mortar bomb. These afflictions left a legacy of debilitating rheumatism and arthritis. After the war Duval slaved for 14 hours a day in a factory, with the threat of dismissal always hanging over him. When a particularly bad bout of rheumatism forced him to take to his bed, he lost his job. He only had one alternative to starvation: theft. At the outset of his new career he managed to 'liberate' a few francs from a railway ticket office. The second attempt resulted in a year in prison.

PREVIOUS PAGE A 1934 photograph showing a part of the main prison building on Devil's Island. The cells with their heavy steel doors face onto the central courtyard, where guards were constantly on duty. The only light and air permitted to the prisoners came through the small grilles above the cell doors.

It was at this time that Duval, influenced by the philosopher Proudhon's dictum that 'Property is theft', developed the theory and practice of 'individual reappropriation'. Theft should not be used for individual enrichment, he argued, but to fund the anarchist revolution. When he was released from prison, Duval became an agitator, visiting factories to stir up class consciousness among the workers, telling them that there was only one answer to violent oppression: violence.

> 'Theft exists only through the exploitation of man by man ... When Society refuses you the right to exist, you must take it ... The policeman arrested me in the name of the Law, I struck him in the name of Liberty.'
>
> Clément Duval, writing in the anarchist newspaper *Révolte*

Duval practised what he preached, and on 25 October 1886 broke into the apartment of a wealthy Parisienne, stealing many valuable items and inadvertently setting the place on fire. It was not long before the police traced the theft back to Duval, and when they came for him and one of them announced 'I arrest you in the name of the law', Duval snapped back 'And I will kill you in the name of freedom.' With that he lunged at the policeman with his knife. The policeman survived his wounds, but Duval was tried, sentenced to death and dragged from the court shouting 'Long live anarchy!' His sentence was subsequently commuted to deportation for life.

On the long voyage to Devil's Island, Duval became acquainted with some of his fellow convicts, and the depths of degradation to which they had been dragged by poverty and ignorance. One of his fellow passengers had killed his mother, another his brother, just for money. A third man had murdered two old women simply so that he could have sex with their corpses. And so it went on. In his memoirs, published in 1929, Duval wrote:

> I would never dare to repeat the experience of the putrid corruption which poisoned every human emotion and sentiment to the last stages of decomposition. Along the walls, lying on their beds made from scraps of material those exhausted people who had said goodbye to all hope ... In hidden corners, where neither the flickering light of the oil-lamps nor the gaze of the curious reached, they were trembling and sobbing; lust showed itself in delirious, bestial fornication. One of Sodom's slums, built in the shade of the well-meaning bourgeoisie's Third Republic, a tribute to their modest morality and their positive penal science.

Once he arrived at *le bagne*, Duval was left in no doubt that rehabilitation was not on the agenda. On Devil's Island men were to be reduced to brute beasts, shackled, beaten, fed rotten food, exposed to every tropical disease. The most vicious prisoners were allowed by the authorities to rise to the top, like scum, while the weakest were simply trodden underfoot. In the midst of this hell on earth, refusing to toady to either the bullies or the authorities, Duval maintained his integrity and his dignity. After eight years on the island, in 1895, he and other anarchists planned a revolt. Duval had the luck to be in a punishment cell when the revolt broke out, for informers had given the guards prior warning. The rebels were mown down without mercy and their bullet-ridden bodies thrown into the sea for the sharks.

All this time, Duval persisted in his attempts to escape, secretly building rafts, stowing away on ships, but never quite managing to get away. But 13 April 1901 turned out to be his lucky day. That night he and eight others slipped away aboard a flimsy canoe and made for the open sea. Despite a storm that threatened to overturn their fragile craft, and waves that almost swamped them, they eventually made it to Dutch Guiana. Still they were not safe: the Dutch authorities would readily extradite them if they received a request from the French. To avoid detection Duval assumed a false name and took on a series of menial jobs, finally working his way to Puerto Rico, from where he set out in June 1903 for the United States. Here, in New York City, he spent the rest of his life, dying in 1935 at the age of 85.

The case of Captain Dreyfus

The most famous prisoner held on Devil's Island was Captain Alfred Dreyfus, a Jewish officer in the French army who in 1894 was accused of passing military secrets to the Germans. He was sentenced to transportation for life, and, despite evidence emerging in 1896 that it was another officer who was culpable, anti-Semitic elements in the army and the Roman Catholic Church launched a rabid campaign against a retrial. Meanwhile, Dreyfus was being held in a small stone hut on Devil's Island, in more or less complete isolation, and when he was falsely reported to have attempted an escape, every night for six weeks he was strapped to his bed by the vicious double buckle. Physically and mentally, Dreyfus said he felt 'nailed to the rack'.

> ‘I will not speak to you of my material circumstances, they are of no interest to me. The physical deprivations ... are nothing. I want only one thing, of which I dream both night and day, and which fills my brain each instant — that my honour, which has never failed me, is restored to me.’
>
> Alfred Dreyfus, letter to Lucie Dreyfus, 20 March 1895

Back in France, Dreyfus had his champions, most notably the novelist Émile Zola, who in 1898 published '*J'Accuse*', a resounding condemnation of the miscarriage of justice that had convicted Dreyfus. The following year, Dreyfus was granted a pardon, freed from Devil's Island and returned to France, but it was not until 1906 that his name was formally cleared.

The real Papillon?

After Captain Dreyfus, the name most closely associated with Devil's Island is that of Henri Charrière, who in his best-selling book *Papillon*, published in 1969 and subsequently turned into a film starring Steve McQueen and Dustin Hoffman, recounted his various attempts in the 1930s and 1940s to escape from *le bagne*. He claims that he was wrongfully convicted for the murder of a pimp, and that he earned his nickname Papillon, meaning butterfly, from the butterfly tattoo on his chest. The story culminates when Charrière jumps from a cliff on Devil's Island into the stormy water carrying a sack of coconuts, which not only keep him afloat but also provide him with liquid sustenance as he drifts for three days under the tropical sun towards the mainland.

As it turned out, Charrière had never been on Devil's Island, and had made his escape from a convict settlement on the mainland. The book was in fact a largely fictional reworking of the adventures of various of his fellow convicts – notably Charles Brunier.

During the First World War Brunier won the Croix de Guerre for gallantry, but in 1923 he was found guilty of murder and sentenced to life on Devil's Island. He escaped three times, the last time at the outbreak of the Second World War, during which he made his way back to Europe and then served with the Free French in Africa. Despite being personally decorated by General de Gaulle and achieving the rank of chief warrant officer, at the end of the war he was sent back to Devil's Island. He was eventually released in 1948. In the old people's home at Domont, near Paris, where he ended his days, the staff said he was a tough old fellow who rarely spoke – except to complain that Charrière had appropriated his story, and to point out the tattoo of a butterfly on his left arm. Brunier died in 2007 at the age of 105 – perhaps the last survivor of the hell that was Devil's Island.

THE END OF DEVIL'S ISLAND

A decree issued on 17 June 1938 ended the transportation of new prisoners to France's penal colonies. However, it was not until 1953 that the last convicts left Devil's Island. Today, the Îles de Salut are being promoted as a luxury resort where the wealthy can spend the winter months in the sun. But few visit Devil's Island, where the fast currents make landing too dangerous. 'I think it's better nobody goes,' a local tourist guide says. 'It has a very bad history. It's out of respect for the past.' The grandson of one convict says that the history of Devil's Island is 'a reminder that the greatest countries – and greatest ideas – can produce horrible monstrosities'.

PATRIOTISM IS NOT ENOUGH

Edith Cavell, executed for helping Allied soldiers to escape, 1915

In the centre of London, just off Trafalgar Square, stands a gaunt memorial featuring a statue of an austere, even stern-looking woman. The plinth underneath the statue, created by Sir George Frampton, bears the following stark inscription:

EDITH CAVELL
BRUSSELS
DAWN
OCTOBER 12
1915

Underneath this are inscribed the words she confided to an Anglican priest on the eve of that fateful dawn: 'Patriotism is not enough. I must have no hatred or bitterness towards anyone.'

Edith Cavell was not quite 50 when she was shot. The daughter of a Church of England vicar, she had worked as a governess until her father became seriously ill, and she gave up her position to look after him. This prompted her to train as a nurse, a career for which she found she had a certain vocation, being both dutiful and kind – if very reserved. Working her way up the nursing hierarchy in a variety of London hospitals, she gradually assumed both managerial and training responsibilities, and in 1907 moved to Brussels, the capital of Belgium, as director of a new nursing school. Her only close companion was Jack, her Jack Russell terrier.

In occupied territory

Following the German invasion of Belgium on 4 August 1914, Cavell's nursing school and its associated clinic were taken over by the Red Cross. After the German First Army marched into Brussels on 16 August, Cavell redirected her energies towards helping Allied servicemen to evade or escape from captivity. She became part of a network of Belgian citizens opposed to the German occupation, and the nursing school and clinic became a refuge for fugitive soldiers, who were often disguised as patients prior to being spirited across the border into the neutral Netherlands.

It was not long before the activities of the network came to the notice of the German authorities, and on 5 August 1915, shortly after the arrest of the resistance leader Philippe Baucq, she and one of her assistants were taken into custody. Other arrests followed, and after a spell in solitary confinement Cavell signed a confession, which also named some of her associates. Apparently her strong religious belief demanded that she always tell the truth; it is also likely that she was unaware of the extremely dangerous consequences that she and her associates faced.

OPPOSITE 'In Memory of the Noblest Type of British Womanhood: Miss Edith Cavell, Died for her Country Oct 12th 1915' – this caption and portrait of Edith Cavell appeared in the *Illustrated London News* following her execution.

ABOVE The execution of Edith Cavell provided a *cause célèbre* for the Allies, and was widely exploited in the press – as can be seen in this contemporary illustration from *Le Petit Journal*.

On 7 October Cavell and eight others faced a German military tribunal, charged with assisting the enemy and undermining the German war effort. The following day, five of them, including Cavell and Baucq, were sentenced to death. The British government claimed to be powerless to help her. 'Any representation from us,' said Lord Robert Cecil at the Foreign Office, 'will do her more harm than good.' The still-neutral Americans tried to intervene via their embassy in Brussels, but were told by the German representative that

> he would rather see Miss Cavell shot than have harm come to one of the
> humblest German soldiers, and his only regret was that they had not 'three or
> four English old women to shoot'.

Death and outrage

While Europe buzzed with diplomatic activity, the German military in Belgium hastened to carry out Cavell's sentence, before the government in Berlin could intervene. They seemed anxious to make an example of this troublesome Englishwoman, and she and Baucq were executed by firing squad at 6 a.m. on 12 October. The German medical officer in attendance was the Expressionist poet (and future Nazi sympathizer) Gottfried Benn, while the German chaplain, Pastor Le Seur, recorded Cavell's last words: 'Ask Father Gahan [the Anglican chaplain in Brussels] to tell my loved ones later on that my soul, as I believe, is safe, and that I am to die for my country.'

Cavell's execution prompted international outrage, and proved something of a propaganda coup for the Allies. They had a new saint and martyr, a woman who had devoted herself to the service of others, slaughtered by the barbarous enemy. Recruitment in Britain was given a boost, and in Berlin the Kaiser, realizing that the Germans had achieved an own goal, ordered that no more women were to be executed without his permission.

After the war Cavell's body was exhumed and brought back to England, where a funeral service was held at Westminster Abbey, before she was finally laid to rest in Norwich Cathedral. Numerous memorials to her were erected around the world, and many streets, hospitals, schools – and even a mountain in the Canadian Rockies – bear her name.

> 'Standing, as I do, in view of God and eternity, I realize that patriotism is not enough. I must have no hatred or bitterness towards anyone.'
>
> Edith Cavell, words to the Revd H. Stirling Gahan, the Anglican chaplain who gave her Holy Communion on the eve of her execution

THE TARTAN PIMPERNEL

IN THE SECOND WORLD WAR, a Church of Scotland minister in occupied France called Donald Caskie helped some 2,000 Allied servicemen to escape. At the outbreak of the war he was minister of the Scots Kirk in Paris, but after the fall of France, having preached against the evils of Nazism, he moved to Marseille, where he set up a safe house for stranded Britons and escaping servicemen at the British Seamen's Mission. Once his activities were discovered, he was arrested and sent to a camp at Grenoble, where he became chaplain to British PoWs and civilian internees. He was arrested once more after he persuaded the Italian commandant to release the civilians before they were transported to Germany. Condemned to die before a firing squad, he was spared following the intervention of Pastor Hans Helmut Peters, a Wehrmacht padre. In 1957 Caskie published *The Tartan Pimpernel*, an account of his wartime adventures.

The King of Handcuffs

Harry Houdini, the greatest escapologist of them all

No escaper has ever matched the celebrity of Harry Houdini, the illusionist and escapologist whose feats earned him the title 'King of Handcuffs'. Such is his fame that his name has been applied to anyone who has performed an ingenious escape, or who has got themselves out of a tight corner. The word 'Houdini' has even made it into the *Oxford English Dictionary*, being used 'to denote an ingenious escape, or a person who embodies the characteristics of Houdini'. As early as 1923 the *New York Times* was explaining that 'Houdini' was also a verb, meaning 'to get out of something, to escape'.

Harry Houdini was the stage name of Ehrich Weiss, a Hungarian-born Jew who in 1878, at the age of four, emigrated with his family to the USA. 'Harry' was an anglicization of 'Ehrie', a familiar form of Ehrich, while 'Houdini' was a tribute to the French illusionist Jean-Eugène Robert-Houdin (1805–71). Houdini began to perform as a magician in 1890 at the tender age of 16 but it was not until he embarked on a four-year tour of Europe in 1900 that his career really started to take off. In each city that he visited he would challenge the local police to strip-search him, put him in handcuffs and leg irons, then lock him in a cell. When a German policeman alleged that he bribed his way to freedom, Houdini sued, and won his case after breaking into the judge's safe – thus demonstrating to the judge that his skill with locks was not counterfeited.

Regurgitations and dislocations

Houdini returned to America rich and famous. He later explained how he dealt with handcuffs and other locks: sometimes by applying force at a certain point, sometimes by using shoelaces or picks or keys, which he would swallow then regurgitate when the need arose. He then began to experiment with straitjackets, having witnessed one in use at an insane asylum in St John's, Nova Scotia:

> I saw a maniac struggling on the canvas padded floor, rolling about and straining each and every muscle in a vain attempt to get his hands over his head and striving in every conceivable manner to free himself from his canvas restraint ... Entranced, I watched the efforts of this man, whose struggles caused the beads of perspiration to roll off him, and from where I stood, I noted that were he able to dislocate his arms at the shoulder, he would have been able to cause his restraint to become slack in certain parts, and so allow him to free his arms ...

He proceeded to apply this observation to a method of escaping from straitjackets or ropes tied round him: as he was bound, he would expand his chest and shoulders by

OPPOSITE Houdini escaping from a straitjacket while suspended from a crane in New York City.

moving his arms slightly away from his body, and then dislocate his shoulders. Initially, he made his escapes behind a screen, but soon realized that it was more dramatic for the audience to witness his struggles in the raw.

Dicing with death

Houdini's audiences soon became jaded and demanded a greater element of danger. Houdini obliged, adding spice to his act by hanging upside down by his ankles high above the ground, while he struggled out of his straitjacket. Then in 1908 he introduced something completely new. It took the form of a metal milk can, large enough to hold a man. It was filled with water, and then Houdini, dressed in a bathing costume, would challenge the audience to hold their breaths while he plunged into the can, which was then topped up to the brim. Long after they were all panting and breathless, Houdini would bob to the surface; after years of training he could hold his breath underwater for three minutes. This was just the warm-up. He then had himself handcuffed and plunged once more into the can, which was topped up again and its lid screwed on and secured with six padlocks. A curtain was then drawn, and three minutes later Houdini would reappear, dripping with water. Then the curtain was drawn back and the can revealed, all of its padlocks still in place. (It was, in fact, a trick can, whose top was only attached to the body by two fake rivets; in addition, the lid was pierced with minute air holes, in case anything should go wrong.)

As the milk-can trick began to attract imitators, Houdini concluded the public could only be satisfied with novelties of an even more sensational sort. In 1912 he tried out a new trick, in which he was handcuffed and put in leg irons, then nailed inside a packing case that was weighed down with 200 lb (90 kg) of lead

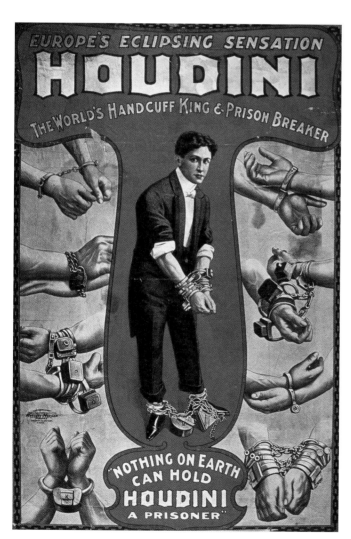

ABOVE A 1906 poster promoting a US tour by Houdini, after his return from Europe.

and lowered under the surface of the East River in New York. In front of an audience of reporters, Houdini reappeared at the surface after only 57 seconds. That same year he introduced the Chinese Water Torture Cell, a glass fronted, water-filled tank in which he was suspended upside down, his ankles locked in a pair of stocks, which were in turn locked to the top of the tank. Houdini's actual escape was performed behind a curtain, and to this day his method remains a mystery.

Ironically enough, it was not one of his acts that killed Houdini – although at least two biopics depict him dying in the Chinese Water Torture Cell. On 22 October 1926 a young student called Whitehead visited Houdini, who was resting on a couch in his dressing room. After the latter had demonstrated the strength of the muscles in his arms, shoulders and back, Whitehead asked him if it was true that punches in the stomach did not hurt him. Houdini conceded that 'his stomach could resist much', at

BURIAL ALIVE

SINCE THE 18TH CENTURY, egged on by Gothic horror tales of premature burial, many people had developed a macabre fear of being buried alive. As a consequence, all kinds of ingenious methods were devised for avoiding this nightmarish fate. In the 1790s, for example, Duke Ferdinand of Brunswick ordered that he was to be buried in a coffin with a window, an air tube and two keys – one to unlock the coffin on the inside, and the other to open the door of the mausoleum. Around the same time a certain Pastor Beck invented a 'safety coffin' from which a tube led to the surface, whose upper end was to be sniffed daily. If no smell of putrefaction was detectable after a few days the coffin was to be dug up and the occupant examined for signs of life. The safety-coffin racket became big business, and in 1822 Dr Adolf Goldsmuth demonstrated the effectiveness of his own version by spending several hours interred in it, during which time he enjoyed a meal of soup, sausage and beer. In 1868 the US inventor Franz Vester came up with a model fitted with an escape hatch and a ladder, and, most importantly, a cord attached to a bell on the surface, by means of which anyone prematurely buried could ring for assistance.

Houdini determined to play on these fears, and for many years worked on an act in which he would escape from the grave. In 1917 he made his first attempt, near Santa Ana in California. Dispensing with a coffin, he had himself manacled and then buried under first one foot, then two feet of earth. That proved easy enough. But when he gradually built up to the customary six feet, he found the weight of earth intolerable, and almost panicked – which would have been disastrous, as panic makes it impossible to conserve air and control one's muscles effectively. He tried to shout, but found his mouth filled with earth. In the end he burrowed upwards enough to break the surface with his hand. Horrified, the onlookers quickly dug out the senseless form of the great escaper. Houdini later noted: 'I tried out "Buried Alive" in Hollywood, and nearly did it. Very dangerous; the weight of the earth is killing.'

which Whitehead delivered a succession of hard blows to the belly of the prostrate Houdini. Then Houdini held up his hand, and a look of extreme pain appeared on his face. He said he had not had time to prepare for the punches. Over the next few days he became seriously ill, running a high temperature. The doctors diagnosed a ruptured appendix, but by the time they removed it, gangrenous peritonitis had set in. In the end the great man conceded defeat: 'I'm getting tired,' he said, 'and I can't fight any more.' He died in the early afternoon of 31 October, in the arms of his wife. 'It was a beautiful sunny day,' one of those present remembered, 'and when the doctor said "He is gone" the heavens clouded over and it poured rain like I have never seen it pour before.'

HOW HOUDINI HELPED BEYOND THE GRAVE

WHILE APPEARING AT THE BIRMINGHAM EMPIRE during a tour of England, Houdini was challenged by an Englishman called Christopher Clayton Hutton to escape from a wooden box that he and a number of associates would construct on stage. Hutton, who had always been fascinated by magicians, illusionists and escapologists, later recalled with some admiration how Houdini had outwitted him by bribing the carpenter, one of the other challengers. The highly eccentric Hutton, known to his colleagues as 'Clutty', found his niche during the Second World War as technical officer to MI9, the British organization that aided Allied servicemen to escape or evade capture in Nazi-occupied Europe, and it was Hutton who devised a whole array of ingenious escape aids for downed airmen (see p. 154).

WHO ELSE WILL TELL THIS STORY?

Six years on the run in Nazi-occupied Europe, 1938–44

'German authorities are now carrying into effect Hitler's oft-repeated intention to exterminate the Jewish people of Europe.' So began a joint declaration issued by eleven Allied governments on 17 December 1942. 'From all the occupied countries,' it continued, 'Jews are being transferred in conditions of appalling horror and brutality to Eastern Europe ... None of those taken away are ever heard of again.'

Just six weeks earlier, on 6 November, Freight Transport No. 42, a train carrying 1,000 Jews, left the holding camp at Drancy on the outskirts of Paris. When Freight Transport No. 42 arrived at Auschwitz some days later, 227 were selected for forced labour (only 4 of whom survived the war); 773, according to the German records, had either died en route or were sent straight to the gas chambers.

Although the German records were normally meticulously accurate, on this occasion there was an error. Two young men, Leo Bretholz and his friend Manfred Silberwasser, had managed to escape from the train. It was neither the first nor the last time that Bretholz had to make a dramatic escape during his many years on the run in Nazi-occupied Europe.

It'll be all right

Leo Bretholz was born in 1921 in a working-class district of Vienna to Polish-Jewish parents. His father Max was a tailor, his mother Dora embroidered brides' dresses. He had two younger sisters, Ditta and Henny. Max Bretholz, who liked to act in the Yiddish theatre, insisted his son learnt modern Hebrew, dreaming that one day they would all settle in Palestine. Max's dream was cut short in 1930 when he died from a perforated ulcer.

> 'We Germans must finally learn not to regard the Jew and members of any organization who have been taught by the Jew as people of our kind ...'
>
> Heinrich Himmler, 5 March 1936

Even before the *Anschluss*, Austria was not a comfortable place for Jews. Leo had to endure many casual taunts: for instance at school, during religious education, Jews were routinely referred to as 'Christ killers'. 'It'll be all right,' said his mother and his aunts and uncles, unable to imagine the horrors ahead. But when Hitler entered Vienna in triumph in March 1938 and the population lined the streets and waved their Nazi flags the hatred came out into the open. Jewish shops were ransacked by Brownshirts, rabbis had their beards set alight, Jewish men and women were forced to scrub the pavements as the Hitler Youth looked on and sneered. Leo's mother saw that it was not, after all, going to be all right. She told Leo it was time to go.

PREVIOUS PAGE A 1938 photograph showing Jews being forced to scrub the streets of Vienna. It was from such humiliations that Leo Bretholz determined to escape.

With his father dead Leo saw himself as the man of the household. He could not desert his family, he said. But – with even his former friends yelling *Saujud*, Jew-pig, in his face, and parks and cinemas and swimming baths all displaying signs saying 'No Jews', and the Brownshirts singing 'When the blood of Jews spurts from the knife' – he had to concede that his mother had a point.

So he got in touch with the Ezra Committee, an organization dedicated to helping German and Austrian Jews escape to Luxembourg, where his Aunt Mina and Uncle Sam had moved shortly after the *Anschluss*. The date set for his departure was 25 October 1938. When the time came to leave, his sister Ditta was quarantined in hospital with scarlet fever. Leo had to say goodbye standing in the rain below her window, using his hands to signal that he was going and that he loved her. She held up a small blackboard on which she'd written in chalk: 'Good luck. We'll be seeing each other soon.'

Across the cold river

'Be careful of the water,' his mother had said. He had told her it was only a shallow river, not like the Danube. A 20-hour train journey had taken him from Vienna to Trier in western Germany, close to the Luxembourg border, and only the River Sauer stood between him and freedom. Now, at an hour before midnight on the last day of October, here he was on the sodden embankment of the Sauer, which had turned into a torrent after a week's heavy rain. It was a moonless, overcast night. As he stepped into the water, the cold took his breath away. He had hoped to wade across, but he was forced to swim, pushing his small case ahead of him. His clothes threatened to drag him under, but he kept his head up and the current helped to take him across. After what seemed like a lifetime, he found himself on the far side. Soon after, he was reunited with his aunt and uncle.

A couple of days later he was picked up in a café by two gendarmes when he failed to produce valid papers. He was told he had three options: return to Germany, face trial in Luxembourg for illegal entry, or take his chances in France or Belgium. Just over the French border, he was told, there was a collective farm of Jewish youths who would help him to get to Paris, where he had relatives.

The two gendarmes who escorted him to the border the next day wished him luck. But it did no good. The youths at the

> '*Only such measures should be taken as will not endanger German life or property (i.e. synagogue burning only if there is no fire-danger to the surroundings) ... Businesses and dwellings of Jews should only be destroyed, not plundered ... As many Jews – especially the well-off ones – are to be arrested as can be accommodated in the available prison space.*'
>
> Orders issued by Reinhard Heydrich to all local Gestapo and SD (SS intelligence) offices, transmitted at 1:20 a.m. on *Kristallnacht*, 10 November 1938.

collective farm could not risk taking him in, they said. They only had temporary visas before they left for Palestine, and the police were always making surprise visits. It would do them no good if they were found sheltering an illegal. Disappointed, Leo sneaked back over the border, and returned to his uncle and aunt's apartment. But all was not lost. The Ezra Committee made arrangements to get him into Belgium on the night of 9 November. As he and other refugees were driven through the dark, they saw the horizon to the east light up with streaks of red and orange. Although they did not know it, they were seeing the distant fires of *Kristallnacht*, the night of broken glass. The synagogues of Germany were being put to the torch.

Calm and storm

Leo ended up in Antwerp, where he resumed his training as an electrician – he had had to abandon his apprenticeship in Vienna – and was delighted to find that all official notices in the post offices were printed not only in Flemish and French, but also in Yiddish. 'I went back to my room,' he remembers, 'and wrote a letter home to my family, telling them that Antwerp felt like Jerusalem.' Even after the Nazis invaded Poland on 1 September 1939 and Britain and France declared war on Germany, Belgium remained neutral, and was little affected during the long months of the Phoney War. Leo carried on with his training, until on 9 May 1940 he was admitted to hospital for a routine operation on a hernia, due to take place the following morning. But when 10 May dawned the air above Antwerp was filled with screaming sirens and the roar of planes and bombs as the Luftwaffe spearheaded the Nazi Blitzkrieg against the Low Countries and France.

The Belgian authorities considered Leo to be an enemy alien. When he reported to the police, as required, he was detained, and with hundreds of others put on board a train. In the chaos of war, they had no idea where they were going. They stopped in Brussels, then continued south into France. In the darkness they could hear planes overhead, and explosions close by. In the morning, as they passed slowly through a station, a man looked into the carriages and made a gesture of a knife cutting a throat. Another night passed, another day. And so it went on. Eventually, on 20 May, they reached their destination, an internment camp at St Cyprien, on the Mediterranean coast close to the Spanish border. They were permitted to walk

> 'Jew haters everywhere. Let there be one Jew, and someone will hate him.'
>
> Comment by one of Bretholz's fellow detainees in France, May 1940

along the beach, but the holiday spirit was missing. Instead, there was just boredom. 'We were a colony of wanderers,' Bretholz recalls, 'beachcombers without destinations, killers of time.'

With the news of the fall of France and the armistice agreed by Marshal Pétain with the Nazis, boredom was replaced by anxiety. What would the French do with their Jews? In August Leo had a visit at the camp from an Antwerp friend, Paul Oesterreicher, who showed Leo how you could just lift up the barbed wire, scoop away some of the sand, and crawl through. No one was looking, no one would notice, no one would particularly care. As it turned out, he was right. Once Leo was out, Oesterreicher put him on a train for Luchon, a spa town in the Pyrenees, close to the Spanish border. Here, showing his Belgian papers, he registered as a legal refugee. He also met up with Jewish friends from Antwerp, including a girl called Anny to whom he'd become close. In November the authorities removed Luchon's Jewish refugees to Bagnères-de-Bigorre, in the Pyrenean foothills not far from Lourdes. Food was becoming scarce, as the Germans requisitioned everything they could get their hands on. Pétain's collaborationist government, from its seat in Vichy, imposed more and more restrictions on France's Jews; and stories were filtering through from the east of deportations and massacres.

> 'All residents of Jewish descent may at any time be forced to live in a specified location by decision of the *Préfet* in the department where they reside.'
>
> Law on Jewish Residents, 4 October 1940, promulgated by the French Vichy government

Leo still lived in hope. Relatives in America were working to get him a visa; he could exchange letters with his mother in Vienna via a cousin in Switzerland; he could hold hands with his girlfriend Anny. In November 1941 the longed-for letter arrived from the States. He was to report to the US consulate in Marseilles to collect his visa, on Monday 8 December. As it turned out, that was the day after Pearl Harbor. 'In view of the hostilities,' he was told when he got there, 'the consulate has been instructed to cease all visa-processing formalities until further notice.'

On the run again

Leo's gloom deepened when news came from Vienna that his mother, sisters, grand-mother and two aunts had been deported. In France, the Vichy government began to assign groups of Jews to specific towns. Leo and Anny and her family were sent to Cauterets, a resort in the mountains to the southwest of Bagnères.

Then the round-ups began. People were being sent to the Parisian suburb of Drancy, and from there, it was said, to the east and who knows what fate. In August 1942 the mayor of Cauterets, an old socialist, let it be known that the authorities were coming for the foreign-born Jews. Anny would be spared, as Belgian Jews were counted as French, but Leo had to hide in the mountains for a couple of days. On his return, Anny's father locked him in a cubbyhole. Then one night a gendarme came looking for him, but Anny said she did not have a key and kept the man at bay. Leo had to look on in fear and impotent rage through the slats of his hiding place as the gendarme pressed himself against his girlfriend and tried to steal a kiss. The man left, but they knew he would be back. Leo had to get out of Cauterets. He walked by night back to Bagnères, and friends there agreed to put him up. They also managed to get some forged ID papers from the Resistance. Leo was to become Paul Meunier

ABOVE French Jews being 'processed' on behalf of the Nazis by French gendarmes.

from Strasbourg, and in this guise was to try to get into neutral Switzerland. He was to travel with the singer Albert Hershkowitz, who was also given a new identity. On 4 October the two of them, with berets on their heads like real Frenchmen, set off on their journey.

Arriving in Evian-les-Bains on Lake Geneva, they met up with the guide who, for a fee of 50 francs per head, was to take them across the mountains to the border with Switzerland. It took them a day and a night. Leo's feet were rubbed raw, his hernia played up. Albert, older and heavier, panted with exhaustion. The guide left them at a stream. *'C'est ici. La frontière,'* he said. Leo grinned, Albert sang snatches of Italian opera. But their joy was short lived. Within half an hour they were intercepted by a Swiss frontier guard. The guard was amiable, but insisted they accompany him to the border post. The sergeant at the border post was far from amiable. He sneered at their false papers. They must go back to France, he said. They pleaded Nazi persecution. It cut no ice. Leo went down on his knees, kissed the man's hand. The man was immovable. Indeed, he seemed to take

> 'Most of you know what it means when a hundred corpses are lying together, when five hundred are lying there, or when a thousand are lying there ... This is an unwritten and never-to-be-written page of glory in our history.'

Heinrich Himmler, speech to SS units, Poland, October 1943

pleasure in their discomfiture. Before long, they found themselves back at the border, where they were handed over to the Vichy police. In the cell where they were kept overnight, Leo tried to peel off his socks, but they had meshed into his bloody feet and the blood had dried around them.

Just four days after leaving Bagnères, Leo and Albert found themselves in the filthy internment camp at Rivesaltes, not far from the camp at St Cyprien from where Leo had escaped two years earlier. He had come full circle. On 20 October they were told they were to be sent to Drancy. They knew this was ominous, but not exactly why; they did not yet realize that Drancy was the last stop before Auschwitz. Leo tried to hide in the ceiling space of his hut, but the guards weren't fooled and told him to stop wasting their time. Knowing the game was up, Leo dropped down, jarring his hernia horribly.

The anteroom of hell

They arrived, 107 of them, at Drancy on 22 October 1942. The French guards issued them with yellow stars, took away their valuables, even photographs of loved ones. They were fed on thin cabbage soup, which gave them chronic diarrhoea. The latrines were open, with no privacy for either men or women, and there was barely any water for washing. They slept on straw scattered on concrete floors. 'What will happen to us?' people constantly asked. Sometimes they asked a different question, equally impossible to answer: 'Where is God?' At night they could hear young children, lying in their own filth, crying for their mothers.

Leo focused on escape. There was no other choice, he had to think about escape, all the time. The only alternative was despair. He was on his own now, he told himself, without mother or sisters or Anny. His chance wasn't long in coming, because it was going to be his last chance. On 5 November they were told to

DRANCY: A SICKNESS OF THE SOUL

ONE PLACE MORE THAN ANY OTHER STANDS AS TESTAMENT to the involvement of French officialdom in the Holocaust. Drancy, a suburb of Paris, was the site of an internment camp where Jews, homosexuals and Gypsies were held in appalling conditions prior to deportation to Auschwitz and other extermination camps. Drancy had originally been built as a large public housing project, intended to house 700 people. As an internment camp, up to 7,000 people lived here at any one time. The camp was opened in August 1941, and was under the control of the French police until July 1943, when the Nazi occupiers took over its administration. In total, 65,000 Jews went through Drancy, of whom only 2,000 survived the war. 'At Drancy,' Bretholz wrote, 'a sickness crept into the soul and never left.'

ABOVE Jews being held at Drancy, near Paris, prior to being deported on board cattle trucks to the extermination camps in the east. At Drancy, Bretholz said, families began to die in each other's presence, and ghosts prematurely haunted the landscape.

gather their belongings. Then their heads were shaved and they were herded onto trucks. Someone started to sing *La Marseillaise*, others joined in, but the singing soon faded away. No one was going to come and save them. At the station Freight Transport No. 42 awaited them. They were ordered to board, *Vite, vite,* quickly, quickly, 50 to each cattle truck, 20 cattle trucks in all. Sometimes children, screaming, were separated from their parents. Inside the trucks there was hardly room to sit or stand, let alone stretch one's legs. They had each been given a little bread and cheese and a tin of sardines, but nothing to drink. There was a bucket in the middle of the floor. This soon filled up. The stench, unrelieved by the two small, barred windows, caused some to vomit. The vomit made the stench worse. 'Where is God?' someone asked yet again. All night the train waited, stationary in a siding. At around nine the next morning, with a judder, the train began to move.

Leo had discussed the possibilities of escape with someone he had met at Drancy, a youth in his late teens called Manfred Silberwasser. Now he stood beside him in the truck, underneath one of the small barred windows. They looked up. That was going to be the way, once it got dark, before they crossed the frontier into Germany. Others in the truck, hearing their conversation, told them they were mad, they would be killed in the fall, or shot by the guards when they were caught, and the rest of them would be killed too, in retaliation. Someone else said they were all going to be killed anyway. Then an old woman pointed her crutch at Bertholz. 'If you jump, maybe you'll be able to tell the story,' she said. 'Who else will tell this story?'

For hours they worked at loosening the bars, sweating, cursing, dry throats burning. All too often their spirits flagged, but in the end the bars bent and moved. After dark, having said farewell to their friends, they hoisted themselves up and out of the narrow gap, and clung onto a ladder that led to the top of the truck. With the wind whistling over their shaved heads, they waited for the right moment. Then the train slowed down for a curve. They took their chance, and jumped.

The kindness of strangers

The German guards must have seen their shadows as they jumped. The train stopped, whistles sounded, there were shouts, shots rang out. Then Leo heard the train pulling away, and he and Manfred found each other in the dark. They began to walk, and when they came to a village they knocked on a door and asked to be taken to the local priest. The priest gave them food and a bed for the night, and sent them on their way early the following morning, before the German patrols came. He gave them the name of a priest in another village, who also gave them food and shelter – and two train tickets for Paris. Leo's mother's youngest sister, Aunt Erna, lived in Paris.

> One should with renewed strength take measures against cruelty to animals ... Special attention is to be devoted to the beef cattle, since through overcrowding in the railway cars great losses have occurred ...
>
> Commander of Police Regiment 25, 11 June 1943

They stayed with Aunt Erna for a fortnight, and acquired new papers. Leo became Marcel Dumont. Then they took a train for the south, and covertly crossed the River Loire into the Vichy zone. There their ways parted. Manfred headed for the Dordogne, where his brother lived. Leo had decided to go back to his friends at Bagnères. Anny might still be living not too far away.

On his way to Bagnères Leo twice managed to give the police the slip. His friends insisted he stay hidden in the house, but Leo, after his escape from the Auschwitz train, had come to believe he led a charmed life, and ignored the advice. On his first outing he was picked up by the police. They were sympathetic, and merely charged him with having left his assigned residence in Cauterets. A lawyer was produced, and advised him to plead guilty and accept the sentence of a year in jail. At least he would be safe from deportation, the man said, and the war might be over by the time he got out. But as they stopped at a café between the court-house in Bagnères and the prison in Tarbes, Leo asked his escort if he could use the lavatory, and then jumped out of the window. His bid for freedom was short-lived, and the guards gave him a vicious beating for getting his escort into trouble. The kicks to his groin, where his untreated hernia lurked, proved particularly painful. After that he was put in solitary confinement for a month.

> In a world in which one cannot trust priests, one might as well flag down the next train to Auschwitz.
>
> Leo Bertholz, *Leap into Darkness* (1999)

In September 1943 Leo was dispatched to a labour camp at Septfonds, north of Toulouse. There he was told he would work hard, but the work would be meaningless. So it turned out: his job was to break big rocks into little rocks. But conditions were better than those he had previously endured, and the

'I was the accuser, God the accused. My eyes were open and I was alone – terribly alone in a world without God and without man.'

Elie Wiesel, *Night* (1958), an account of his experiences during the Holocaust. Bretholz too felt that 'God seemed to have washed his hands of the Jews.'

guards sympathetic. They would chat, and bring the prisoners water as they worked.

His friend Manfred, with whom he had jumped from the train, came to visit. They talked through the barbed wire. Manfred said he could get Leo papers, if he could escape. In mid-October Leo was told he was to be sent to the Atlantic coast, to build fortifications. He and a group of other prisoners were put aboard a train in Toulouse. The guards stayed on the platform, so Leo simply opened the window on the other side of the carriage and dropped down onto the tracks, before the train even left the station. Grimacing with the jolt to his hernia, he caught a bus to Blagnac, on the northern outskirts of Toulouse, where he was taken in by friends of his Aunt Erna. He wrote to Manfred, and shortly afterwards received a new birth certificate. He was now Max Henri Lefèvre. It was the last he ever heard from Manfred. On Christmas Eve he was back at his Aunt Erna's apartment in Paris.

A time to fight

While he stayed with his aunt in Paris he received a letter from Anny. She and her family were now in the village of Châlus, near Limoges in central France. On 2 March 1944 Leo set off to see her again. But when he got there, the atmosphere was strained. Why hadn't he come for her in Nice, she demanded. She'd written to him that she was sheltering in a convent there. He was in prison then, he said. Besides, in Nice they pulled down your trousers if they thought you looked even the least bit Jewish and if you had no foreskin they shot you on the spot. That was what he'd heard.

Too many friends and relatives had gone. The war and the Nazis and their toadying Vichy friends had gnawed like rats at normal, decent human feelings, feelings that only ended up betraying you. Leo had seen too many men and women miss their chance to make a break because they would not be parted from their loved ones. He had not, would not, make that mistake. Attachments like that only got you killed. In April he left Anny and her family and went to Limoges to join the Resistance.

The group he joined was a Jewish organization called *Le Sixième*, the sixth. The name distinguished them from the Fifth Columnists, the collaborationists who worked for the Nazis. *Le Sixième* specialized in forging papers, helping those on the run, working to reunite families. Leo acquired the uniform of the Compagnons de France, a Vichy paramilitary youth organization, which gave him cover – although once, while observing a train full of deportees, he was held and questioned by the SS before being slapped about the face and released.

On a mission one day in May 1944 Leo's hernia almost killed him. He was in a park, and collapsed on a bench in agony. The bulge in his groin was growing larger and larger. His hernia had become strangulated, and unless it was operated on immediately he would die. A passerby called an ambulance. Leo knew nothing until he woke up in hospital the following morning. He could tell he had had the operation from the drainage tube in his groin. They would have seen that he was circumcised. Then a nun peered down at him. She said she was Sister Jeanne d'Arc. Joan of Arc? He must still be dreaming, he thought. She said that as long as she was on the ward, he had nothing to fear. She was as good as her word, and kept him safe until he was discharged at the end of May. Within a week the Allies had landed in Normandy, but this did not stop the killings and deportations. One of Leo's colleagues was caught with incriminating evidence on him and got two bullets in the head.

> "You have family?" he asked. I shrugged because I no longer knew.
>
> Leo Bertholz, *Leap into Darkness* (1999)

In mid-August the Resistance rose up in Limoges, taking the entire German garrison prisoner. *Le Sixième* continued its work, trying to trace fathers, mothers, daughters, sons, sisters, brothers. When the end of the war in Europe came, Anny and her family announced they were going back to Belgium. Leo had reapplied to emigrate to America. Eventually he got his visa, and sailed on 19 January 1947, arriving in New York ten days later. He'd heard that Anny had got engaged. There was nothing to keep him in Europe.

In Baltimore Leo met up with several of his surviving aunts and uncles. But there were other uncles and aunts and cousins who were not there, who were nowhere. Their final destination had been Auschwitz. Some years later Leo made a return visit to Europe with his wife Flo and met up with his cousin Sonja. She had been the last to see Leo's mother, and Sonja said she had been happy – happy that her son was safe. It was only in 1962 that Leo received definitive confirmation of the fate of his mother and his sisters, Henny and Ditta. On 9 April 1942 they had been sent to the Jewish ghetto in Izbica, Poland – a staging post on the journey to oblivion. They were not numbered among the few who had returned.

> It was a terrible time through which I was living. The war raged about us, and nobody knew whether or not he would be alive the next hour.
>
> Anne Frank, diary entry, 25 March 1944. Anne Frank died in Belsen in March 1945, at the age of 15.

It was many years before Leo Bretholz could bring himself to speak about his experiences. But bit by bit he began to unburden himself about his years on the run to Michael Olesker, a Baltimore journalist, and this resulted in their moving, gripping account, *Leap into Darkness*, published in 1999. 'Forgetting, or not speaking,' Bretholz maintains, 'means that we've been silenced, which is what Hitler wanted.'

SNATCHING GLORY OUT OF DEFEAT

The British army is rescued from Dunkirk, 1940

Once the northern French harbour town of Dunkerque – Dunkirk to the English – was known as a haunt of pirates and privateers. Today, as well as being one of France's busiest ports, it attracts thousands of holidaymakers to its beaches and dunes, lured by its surf and its sand. But during the Second World War the place acquired an entirely different significance, when, between 26 May and 4 June 1940, a third of a million Allied troops, the majority of them British, were evacuated from inlets, jetties and beaches around Dunkirk, while under constant bombardment by the Luftwaffe. It was the greatest maritime evacuation in history, and the bulk of the British army was saved to fight another day.

It was by no means a victory. The Nazis went on to overrun France, which, believing itself deserted by its British ally, agreed to an armistice. It was to be another four years before the British, with their Commonwealth and US Allies, were to return to liberate France. And yet to many in Britain it was a triumph, and did much to forge a sense of unity of purpose. Perhaps only the British can, in J.B. Priestley's words, snatch glory out of defeat.

The *Sichelschnitt*

The Allies had not been prepared for the audacity of the German invasion plan, the offensive in the west that ended the long, expectant months of the Phoney War. While German Army Group C engaged the French holding the Maginot Line – the system of French fortifications along the German border – Army Group B had, on 10 May 1940, penetrated deep into the Netherlands and Belgium, drawing the French First and Ninth Armies, together with the British Expeditionary Force (BEF) under General Gort, north. It proved to be a massive feint. Rundstedt's Army Group A, positioned in the German centre, now did what none of the Allied commanders had conceived possible: it punched in force through the rugged, mountainous terrain of the Ardennes, the sector where the French defences were at their weakest, and by 14 May General Guderian's Panzers had crossed the River Meuse. This *Sichelschnitt* ('cut of the scythe') proved to be a masterstroke. The Maginot Line was bypassed, and by 20 May Guderian's Panzers had reached the Channel coast at Abbeville, cutting off the rear of the French and British armies fighting in Belgium.

The Allied commanders, especially the defeatist 68-year-old Maurice Gamelin, the French commander-in-chief, had relied on strong static deployments, and were mentally unprepared to deal with the fast-moving Blitzkrieg tactics of Rundstedt and

OPPOSITE A long line of soldiers snakes across the beaches of Dunkirk waiting to be picked up by the 'little ships'.

Guderian, in which tanks and air power were used to cut the enemy's support lines. On 19 May Gamelin was replaced by the 73-year-old Maxime Weygand, an even older, even gloomier general, whose first act was to inform the French prime minister, Paul Reynaud, that there was no hope of beating back the Germans. A spirited British counterattack at Arras on 21 May proved unsuccessful. Winston Churchill, who had replaced Neville Chamberlain as British prime minister on 10 May, the day the German campaign had started, ordered the BEF to withdraw to the coast and await evacuation.

A fatal decision

As the scattered and demoralized units of the BEF, together with large numbers of French troops, made for Dunkirk, Gort organized a last line of defence to cover the evacuation, along the Aa Canal and the Scarpe and Yser rivers. He had no great hope that he could hold out against Guderian's Panzers, but on 24 May he was saved by an extraordinary decision by Hitler, who sent Guderian an order to halt. 'Führer is terribly nervous,' General Franz Halder had already recorded on 17 May. 'Frightened by his own success, he is afraid to take any chance and so would rather pull the reins on us.' A few days later Halder, the chief of staff of the German army, reported: 'Führer keeps worrying about the southern flank. He rages and screams that we are on the way to ruin the whole campaign. He won't have any part in continuing the operation in a westward direction.'

> My first impression of the coast was a beautiful stretch of sand, with what looked like shrubs on the beach, until they all started moving into lines.

Stoker Arnold Saunders of the destroyer HMS *Jaguar* recalls the scene at Bray-Dunes beach on 28 May 1940

It seems Hitler wanted to preserve his armour for an expected French counter-attack in the south. Other theories have also been put forward. One suggests that Goering persuaded Hitler that the Luftwaffe (more pro-Nazi than the conservative army generals) should have the honour alone of annihilating the British. Another proposes that Hitler calculated that the British would be more likely to sue for peace if their army was allowed to return home unscathed. Whatever the reason, Hitler's 'Halt' order allowed the BEF to escape, despite the depredations of the Luftwaffe.

The little ships

The troops dribbling and then pouring into Dunkirk were exhausted, hungry, footsore and demoralized, and relations between French and British commanders were tetchy, to say the least. Despite the fact that Hitler had held back his main armour, masses of well-equipped German infantry were pressing at the perimeter defences of the port, set up along the line of a number of canals: some German troops attempted to cross over a bridge dressed as nuns, others hid themselves among horses and cattle, others tried to cross by boat.

The organization of the evacuation from Dunkirk, codenamed Operation Dynamo, was entrusted to Vice Admiral Bertram Ramsay, Royal Navy flag officer at Dover. The evacuation had begun on the evening of 26 May, with cross-Channel ferries taking men from the quays of Dunkirk. They were joined by British and French destroyers, which took men from the mole protecting the harbour. But it was soon realized that these vessels were not going to be sufficient to withdraw all the troops; smaller vessels with shallow draughts would be needed to get tens of thousands of men off the beaches. On 14 May the BBC had broadcast an appeal for the owners of small boats to register their vessels with the Admiralty, and on 27 May the owners were informed that their vessels were to be commandeered, and that they were to take them to assembly points at Sheerness and Ramsgate. At this stage, none of them were told of the purpose of this exercise.

> 'It was the queerest, most nondescript flotilla that ever was, and it was manned by every kind of Englishman, never more than two men, often only one, to each small boat. There were bankers and dentists, taxi drivers and yachtsmen, longshoremen, boys, engineers, fishermen and civil servants ...'
>
> Arthur D. Divine, who manned one of the 'little ships'

In all, hundreds of 'little ships' – fishing boats, barges, yachts, pleasure cruisers and other small craft – answered the call, and 588 of them were deemed seaworthy enough to take part in the evacuation. Lieutenant A. Dann, who accompanied the first convoy to Dunkirk, described the range of vessels that made up this 'miniature armada':

> A dozen or so motor yachts from 20 to 50 feet [6 to 15 m] in length, nicely equipped and smartly maintained by proud individual owners, a cluster of cheap 'conversion jobs' mainly the work of amateur craftsmen, who had set to work in their spare time to convert a ship's lifeboat or any old half discarded hull into a cabin cruiser of sorts ... half a dozen Thames river launches resembling nothing so much as the upper decks of elongated motor buses with their rows of slatted seats, but given a tang of the waterside by rows of painted lifebuoys ... The very names of the latter craft are redolent of the quiet of Richmond, Teddington and Hampton Court: *Skylark*, *Elizabeth* and *Queen Boadicea*. A strange flotilla indeed to be taking an active part in what has been described as the greatest naval epic in history.

The route they had to follow – a round trip of some 175 miles (280 km) – was an indirect one, a giant dogleg due east towards the Belgian coast, and then southwest to Dunkirk, so avoiding the German guns at Calais and Gravelines. The first flotilla arrived off the French coast around noon on 29 May. There seemed to be a low bank of cloud along the coast, but this turned out to be smoke from the burning town. A pair of German planes flew low over the sea, firing their machine guns. The skipper of the *Seasalter*, a smack used for dredging oyster beds near Burnham-on-Crouch in Essex, described what they saw as they approached the shore:

> The soldiers were coming off the beach clinging to bits of wood and wreckage and anything that would float. As we got close enough we began to pick them up. We saw a row-boat coming off loaded right down with troops. And with this we went to and fro, bringing as many as it would dare hold, and in the meantime we went round picking up as many as we could. When we got a load we would take them off to one of the ships lying off in the deep water.

'The little ships, the unforgotten Homeric catalogue of *Mary Jane* and *Peggy IV*, of *Folkestone Belle*, *Boy Billy* and *Ethel Maud*, of *Lady Haig* and *Skylark* … the little ships of England brought the Army home.'

Philip Guedalla, *Mr Churchill* (1941)

On the beaches

The thousands of men on the beaches maintained their orderly queues across the sands and into the water, or along the great mole of Dunkirk harbour. Only occasionally did discipline break down, for example when French troops sought to board a ship intended for British soldiers, or vice versa. Here and there along the beaches, lorries had been driven out to form improvised jetties, with planks extending from roof to roof; but mostly the men had to wade. Private Robert Holding of the Royal Sussex Regiment recalled how the boats came 'as close to the column heads as possible':

> The queue edged its way forward till the leaders, chest-deep in water, were pulled aboard and ferried out to the ship. Unhurriedly and calmly the boats plied back and forth, carrying as many men as they could safely cram aboard, but never seeming to make any impression on the endless queue which edged forward continuously …

The orderly calm was frequently shattered by the Luftwaffe, most terrifyingly by the Stukas, the German dive bombers that accompanied their attacks on the ships off shore and on the men on the beaches with a siren scream. 'You felt so completely exposed on the beach,' Gunner Lieutenant Elliman remembered. 'The Stukas were diving, zooming, screeching and wheeling over our heads like a flock of huge infernal seagulls.' When an attack came, the men scattered, then as quickly formed up again for fear of losing their place in the queue. When night came, sleep proved impossible. 'It was just waiting, waiting, waiting,' Elliman recalled. The troops on the ground felt bitterly let down that there was no sign of the RAF. In fact RAF fighters *were* in action, unseen above the low cloud; 145 of them were lost during the operation.

In the stress and the chaos of the evacuation there were many tragedies, not all of them inflicted by the enemy. One such incident took place when men were trying to board a destroyer from the volunteer motor launch *Advance*. As they scrambled up the nets lowered over the side, the destroyer, coming under air attack, jerked forward without warning and several men were crushed between the destroyer's side and the *Advance*'s port quarter. One dark night, further out to sea, the minesweeper HMS *Lydd* mistook the *Comfort*, a British drifter, for a German MTB (motor torpedo boat), rammed it and split it in half. When survivors tried to clamber up the side of the minesweeper they were taken for a German boarding party, and, as *Lydd*'s commander later reported, 'Fire was therefore opened with rifles.'

'The din was infernal. The 5.9 batteries shelled ceaselessly and brilliantly. To the whistle of shells overhead was added the scream of falling bombs. Even the sky was full of noise – anti-aircraft shells, machine-gun fire, the snarl of falling planes, the angry hornet noise of dive bombers.'

Arthur D. Divine

By far the greatest damage was inflicted by the enemy: on 29 May alone ten destroyers, eight other ships and a host of smaller craft were sunk, mostly by the Luftwaffe, though U-boats and German MTBs were also out hunting in the Channel. Another nine ships were lost on 1 June. The casualties were appalling. Men were drowned, burnt, broken, dismembered. On the beaches the soft sand helped to absorb the blasts of the bombs, but when Messerschmitts came strafing with their machine guns, they left a trail of carnage. 'There were,' Major Colvin of the Grenadier Guards recalled, 'many unpleasant sights of wounded men left on the sands to die, or be drowned by the flood tide.' Those wounded men who did get away often had to wait days before they were treated. By this time, many wounds had become infested with maggots, or infected with gangrene.

The rearguard

All this time the pocket around Dunkirk was coming under ever increasing pressure, as the heavily armed German infantry closed in. Within the perimeter, there were disagreements at the highest level between the French and the British about the latter's role in fighting a rearguard action to cover the evacuation. The French understood that Gort had ordered General Harold Alexander, in command of the British rearguard, to support them with three divisions, but Alexander denied he had had any such order. His job, he said, was to evacuate all his men. A tense meeting on 31 May ended with Admiral Abrial, the senior French officer in Dunkirk, making a defiant declaration to Alexander:

Since we cannot count on English cooperation, General, I will fulfil my mission using French troops. We French have a mission which is to fight to the last man to save as many soldiers as possible from Dunkirk. Until we have achieved this goal, we will remain at our posts.

ABOVE Chaos and desperation on the streets of Dunkirk.

While French units were still making their way towards Dunkirk, the French were determined to go on fighting.

Among the British units holding the perimeter that day was a group of Grenadier Guards holed up in a cellar while shells fell all about them. On a wireless they heard that two-thirds of the army had been evacuated. 'In the gloom,' Signalman George Jones recalled,

> ... looks and silence betrayed the thoughts of every one of us. Here we were miles inland, and virtually trapped in a town collapsing from bombardments from both sides. Meanwhile the best part of the army was safely back in England. It felt very lonely.

Their dark mood was short-lived, however, when they received the order to go that night to the beaches.

The following day, 1 June, had been intended by the British as the last day of the evacuation. But the French were not happy with this, and Churchill himself decided that 'The success or failure of our efforts to rescue the remnants of the French Army might have great results for the Alliance.' He therefore ordered that the evacuation continue as long as the perimeter front was held – 'even at the cost of naval losses'.

That day, 1 June, saw the Germans break through the perimeter at a number of locations. There followed a desperate fighting retreat by the BEF rearguard, some units only withdrawing when their ammunition ran out. One eyewitness, the war diarist of 3 Brigade, described the landscape through which they made their way towards the beaches:

> The scenery provided a ... picture of the abomination of desolation. Ruined and burnt out houses ... vehicles abandoned, many of them charred relics of twisted metal on the roadside and overturned in the ditches ... Horses dead or dying from want of water. Here and there civilian or French Army corpses lying in the open ...

With the rate of evacuation slowed by the shipping losses on 1 June, Alexander now told the French that he intended to hold an inner perimeter line until the night of 2–3 June. That night, at around 11 p.m., the last ships carrying BEF soldiers sailed from Dunkirk. Alexander then set off in a motorboat to inspect the beaches and harbour, to make sure no British soldier was left behind. At 11.30 p.m. Captain Bill Tennant, the senior Royal Navy officer in Dunkirk, sent a message to Ramsay in Dover: 'BEF evacuated.'

It was not quite the end. The British had been covered by some 25,000 French troops, and Admiral Abrial requested that 'the rearguard should not be sacrificed'. Churchill, although irritated by the inefficiency with which the French had organized the evacuation of their own troops, agreed. At 10 o'clock on the morning of 3 June Ramsay, declaring 'We cannot leave our allies in the lurch', ordered that his ships go back for the French on the night of 3–4 June.

The French mounted a desperate counterattack on the morning of 3 June. It failed to achieve its objectives, but served to hold up the German advance. That evening, French units were gradually withdrawn from the inner perimeter. The last troops were ordered to hold their positions until the early

> 'Entire columns of soldiers had been annihilated by the bombardment. Not far from Bastion 32 lay a line of corpses who had fallen on top of each other; it was if a gust of wind had blown over a row of wooden soldiers. The dark road was so full of obstructions that it was impossible to avoid some of the corpses, which were run over by my car.'
>
> Commandant René Lehr of the French army, describing the night of 2–3 June in Dunkirk

hours of 4 June – unless the Germans attacked, in which case they were to stay and put up a fight. As more and more men converged on the embarkation quays and the beaches, one French general described the spectacle as 'a human tide ... following its nose to safety'. Yet discipline was maintained: when, in the early hours of 4 June another French general marched along the pier to board the last British motorboat to leave Dunkirk, a thousand men stood to attention as he passed. Later that morning, these men, together with 40,000 other French troops, were taken prisoner when the

Germans entered the town. One German staff officer complained that, although it was so hot, he and his fellow officers could not swim in the sea: there was too much oil from sunken ships, and too many corpses.

The spirit of Dunkirk

In all, over 100,000 French troops had been evacuated, together with a quarter of a million British and Commonwealth soldiers. But not all of the BEF escaped: some 140,000 British troops remained in France after 4 June, including the entire 51st Highland Division, which had supported the French on the Maginot Line. It was eventually forced to surrender on 12 June. Ten days later the new prime minister of France, Marshal Philippe Pétain, signed an armistice with the Germans, rejecting a proposal from Churchill that Britain and France should form a political union to combat Hitler. Such a union would be 'a union with a corpse,' he said. 'Better to be a Nazi province.'

But Britain was not a corpse. Its army had survived, although it had had to abandon much of its heavy equipment and transport at Dunkirk, and the troops themselves were demoralized and disillusioned with their generals. Churchill himself told the House of Commons on 4 June that 'We must be very careful not to assign to this deliverance the attributes of a victory. Wars are not won by evacuations.' And yet, he continued, the British would not give in:

> Even though large tracts of Europe and many old and famous states have fallen or may fall into the grip of the Gestapo and all the odious apparatus of Nazi rule, we shall not flag or fail. We shall fight in France, we shall fight on the seas and oceans, we shall fight with growing confidence and growing strength in the air, we shall defend our island, whatever the cost may be, we shall fight on the beaches, we shall fight on the landing grounds, we shall fight in the fields and in the streets, we shall fight in the hills; we shall never surrender.

The following day, the writer J.B. Priestley gave one of his regular radio talks on the BBC. On this occasion, he paid tribute to the 'little ships' of Dunkirk, particularly those that did not come back:

> Among those paddle steamers that will never return was one that I knew well, for it was the pride of our ferry service to the Isle of Wight ... But now – look – this little steamer, like all her brave and battered sisters, is immortal. She'll go sailing proudly down the years in the epic of Dunkirk. And our great-grand-children, when they learn how we began this war by snatching glory out of defeat, and then swept on to victory, may also learn how the little holiday steamers made an excursion to hell and came back glorious.

Thus the 'Dunkirk spirit' – that stubborn defiance of all those who would crush the proud spirit of a free people – entered into the mythology of what it means, to many, to be British.

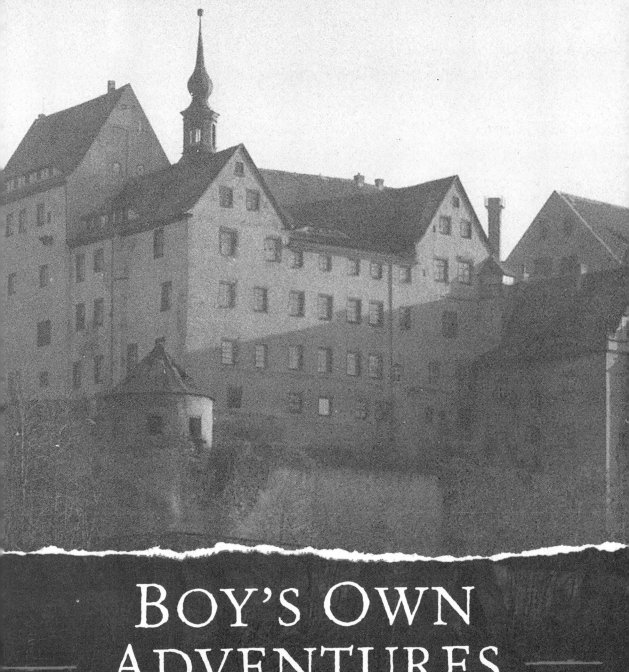

Boy's Own Adventures

Escapades at Colditz Castle, 1940–5

There is one name above all others that conjures up an image of gallant Allied officers making attempt after attempt to escape the Germans: Colditz. The infamous and forbidding castle stands on a rock above the town of the same name near Leipzig in eastern Germany. Although the castle dates back to the 11th century, much of the present edifice was built in the 16th, with further additions in the 19th, when the castle became first a workhouse for the poor and then an asylum for the 'incurably insane'. Because it was thought to be exceptionally secure, during the Second World War Colditz was designated as Oflag IV-C, a prisoner-of-war camp. It was no ordinary prisoner-of-war camp, however, but a *Sonderlager*, a high-security prison, for those officers – British and Commonwealth, Polish, French, Dutch, Belgian, Yugoslav, American – who had proved to be incorrigible escapers.

But Colditz wasn't a punishment camp, and indeed many thought it more comfortable than other camps they'd been in. With such determined and ingenious inmates, it was perhaps not surprising that Oflag IV-C turned out to be anything but escape-proof, and devising, planning and executing escape schemes occupied a considerable amount of the prisoners' time. Various boisterous sports, and a lot of amateur theatricals, also helped while away the hours, and in pursuit of these entertainments the prisoners were allowed to borrow tools from their captors, on the gentlemanly understanding that they would not be used for escape attempts. Some of the younger men found 'goon-baiting' (winding up the guards) a good way of letting off steam – dropping water bombs from high windows was particularly popular – and for many the whole experience cannot have been that different from their boyhood years at boarding school. One of the German officers on the staff later talked of 'the unruly mob of prisoners we had at Colditz'. Another, Captain Reinhold Eggers, a former schoolmaster who was in charge of security, said he felt like 'a teacher dealing with a lot of unruly boys'. After the war, many of his former charges welcomed him warmly when he visited England.

> ‘I think it was the most comfortable prisoner-of-war camp in Germany, because we weren't terribly crowded (except at the very end). It was a nice castle and not a nasty hutted thing in the middle of a swamp.’
>
> Edward Davis-Scourfield, an inmate at Colditz, quoted in S.P. Mackenzie, *The Colditz Myth* (2004)

PREVIOUS PAGE During the Second World War, Colditz Castle became Oflag IV-C, a high-security prison for Allied officers who had proved particularly troublesome to the Germans.

Stubborn, proud and uncompromising

A neutral Swiss inspector found in Colditz 'an excellent elite of remarkably strong characters, stubborn, proud and uncompromising'. They were not just regular service officers, but came from a great variety of backgrounds – teachers, academics, lawyers, engineers, writers, actors, farmers, industrialists, and so on. Lieutenant-Commander William Lawton Stephens of the Royal Naval Volunteer Reserve, who was at Colditz in 1942, recalls: 'The morale and spirit of the prisoners was very high indeed and I suppose that almost every prisoner who was there was trying in one way or another to escape.'

Things had to be organized along proper military lines, however, with liaison between the various nationalities and an orderly method established 'to give everyone a chance':

> Each nationality had an escape committee of five or six officers, who entirely controlled the escape attempts of that nationality; then, in addition each nationality appointed a representative for an international escape committee, who decided which country should be the next in turn to try a scheme.

The national escape committees devised rotas, giving priority to those who had been longest in the camp, and to those who would be most valuable to the war effort should they succeed in getting home. 'The only means of short-circuiting this rota system,' Stephens recalled, 'was to think of a scheme for getting out, and if this was approved by the committee one would then be given the opportunity of trying it oneself.'

Audacity, ingenuity and enterprise

Most escape attempts from Colditz – including at least two involving tunnels – did not succeed, but many of them were nevertheless remarkable for their sheer cheek. This is particularly true of those who tried to walk out of the castle in disguise. One French lieutenant dressed himself up as a woman, while another pretended to be the camp's German electrician, and was only caught when he was unable to produce an official exit token. After Lieutenant Airey Neave (later to become a prominent Tory MP) had been caught in August 1941 in the uniform of a German corporal, one of the more humorous of the German officers, Captain Paul Priem, announced at the next roll call that 'Corporal Neave is to be sent to the Russian front.' The prisoners loved the joke and fell about laughing. In January 1942 Neave's third attempt was

> ‘To maintain discipline they [the Wehrmacht staff] don't resort to a weak man's refuge, petty tyranny; but treat us – after they have taken every precaution to prevent us escaping – as gentlemen who know the meaning of honour, and possess a gentleman's dignity.’
>
> Padre Ellison Platt, quoted in Margaret Duggan (ed.), *Padre in Colditz* (1978)

Tunnel to oblivion

OWING TO A MISCALCULATION, one attempt to tunnel out of Colditz came to a premature end in the commandant's wine cellar. The commandant was something of a connoisseur, and the cellar was full of rare and expensive wines. The would-be escapers consoled themselves by downing the contents of a hundred or so bottles, and then refilled them with the contents of their bladders, prior to pushing the corks back in and replacing the bottles on the shelves.

successful, and later that year a group of five men got out disguised as German officers and Polish orderlies, two of them finally reaching Switzerland.

In April 1943 Lieutenant Mike Sinclair tried to pass himself off as one of the senior German guards, Sergeant Major Fritz Rothenberger, nicknamed 'Franz Josef' from his close resemblance to the former Austrian emperor. Despite his fluent German, false moustache, perfect uniform and close study of Rothenberger's mannerisms, movements and speech, Sinclair was foiled when the real Rothenberger appeared in person, leading to some initial confusion on the part of the guards. Sinclair – known as the 'Red Fox of Colditz' because of his numerous attempts to escape – was shot dead in September 1944 after climbing over the wire in the exercise park. He had been ordered to stop several times before the guards opened fire, and was killed by a bullet that ricocheted off his elbow into his heart. The Germans buried him with full military honours.

Late in 1940 Peter Allan, dressed in a Hitler Youth uniform, had himself sewn into a mattress, one of several that the Germans were moving to another camp. Once he was out of the castle and deposited in an empty house in the town, he cut himself out. Allan eventually made his way to Vienna, where he failed to secure asylum in the (still neutral) American consulate, and was returned to Colditz. In September 1942 Dominic Bruce hid inside a packing case intended for excess belongings, and then climbed down from a storeroom window on knotted bed sheets – having scrawled a message in German for his captors on the now-empty box: 'The Colditz air no longer agrees with me. Goodbye!' He was arrested a week later in the Baltic port of Danzig, trying to board a ship to neutral Sweden.

Perhaps the most remarkable escape plan was that involving the 'Colditz Cock'. This was a two-man glider built by Bill Goldfinch and Jack Best, two RAF pilots, in the attic above the castle's chapel. The idea was to launch it from the roof by means of a pulley system and fly across the River Mulde, some 200 feet (60 m) below. The plan might well have succeeded had not the war come to an end before it could be put into practice.

Most of the successful escapes were more straightforward – but equally daring. For example, in August 1941 two Dutch officers hid under a manhole cover in the

ABOVE One of the more remarkable escape plans involved the building of a glider known as the 'Colditz Cock', part of which is seen here in the attic above the castle's chapel.

exercise area until dark, then slipped away, reaching the Swiss border by train. That same year three French lieutenants escaped while visiting the town dentist, and a fourth vaulted over a wire and cycled all the way to Switzerland. In 1942 Pat Reid and three others got out via the PoW kitchens, and they too all made it to Switzerland. (After the war Reid wrote two accounts of life in the castle, and of the various escape attempts – including his own. These became the basis of the 1955 film *The Colditz Story*, with John Mills playing Reid, and also inspired a long-running television series in the 1970s. It was largely via these channels that Colditz became an icon in British popular culture.)

Safer inside than out

Given the provocation they were frequently subjected to, the Wehrmacht guards in Colditz behaved throughout the war with admirable restraint; remarkably, Mike Sinclair was the only man ever killed trying to escape from the castle. However, as the war drew to a bloody close, the Nazi leadership, reeling from defeat after defeat, became increasingly vindictive towards escaped prisoners, and it is likely that the Canadian officer Bill Millar, who in January 1944 became the last man to make it out of Colditz, was secretly killed by the SS – a foretaste of the terrible retribution visited on the 'Great Escapers' of Stalag Luft III shortly afterwards (see pp.148-9). As a consequence, the SBO (senior British officer) in Colditz issued an order forbidding further escape attempts. It was no longer a game.

By April 1945, with the Third Reich collapsing in flames and the fighting coming

> We continued to fight in Colditz. We were the besiegers within and we were holding down a large number of troops outside.

Pat Reid, who escaped from Colditz in 1942; quoted in Walter Morrison, *Flak and Ferrets* (1995).

nearer and nearer to Colditz, the SBO successfully prevented the transfer of his men elsewhere. He had realized it would be much safer inside Colditz with the Wehrmacht than outside, at the mercy of the SS and the Gestapo in terminally murderous mood. The Wehrmacht guards maintained a visible presence at the Castle, but mainly to show the SS troops in the town below that all was as it should be.

Liberation came on 16 April 1945, when US forces entered the castle after a two-day fight. One inmate, Hugh Bruce, remembered the reaction when the first GI came through the gate: 'A great cheer went up, and the bewildered and uneasy soldier stepped back as the jubilant crowd surged forward to embrace him.' Suddenly, a lot of tensions were released. 'It was pure wild west,' recalled another inmate, Dominic Bruce, 'and we all got guns and went off and liberated chickens and bottles of wine which had been suffering under Hitler.' More sombrely, some of the former prisoners visited a nearby concentration camp holding Hungarian Jews. It was only then that they realized quite how lucky they had been.

OTHER RANKS AT COLDITZ

POW CAMPS WERE GENERALLY DIVIDED between those for officers and those for other ranks. Under the Geneva Convention, officers were considered gentleman and therefore not expected to undertake menial work. This did not apply to other ranks, and many captured Allied servicemen found themselves working on farms or down mines. It was thus considered a 'cushy billet' to get the job as an orderly in an officers' camp. However, class antipathy sometimes bubbled up to the surface. One ranker, Maurice Newey, remarked of the officers in Colditz: 'They had all the advantages, a much better education than the rank and file, better food and were able to buy things they needed to help their escape.' He added: 'They were brave men, however, who did escape.' Another ranker, Alec Ross, who was personal batman in Colditz to Douglas Bader, the famous legless fighter pilot, was told in 1943 that as a member of the Royal Army Medical Corps he was to be repatriated. Bader blocked the move, saying 'He came here as my lackey and he'll stay as my lackey.' Consequently, Ross recalls, 'I had to stay another two bloody years ...' At one point in Colditz the orderlies, fed up with the high-handedness of the officers, actually went on strike. But when Captain Eggers, the German security officer, offered a transfer to one disgruntled orderly if he were to spy on his superiors, the man turned him down flat. 'I may not like it here,' he said defiantly, 'but I am still British.'

CLIMBING THE
— DIAMOND —

Three Italian PoWs attempt an ascent of Mount Kenya, 1943

Felice Benuzzi had been a colonial officer in Abyssinia when British forces invaded in 1941. Along with ten thousand other Italians, Benuzzi found himself interned in PoW Camp 354 near Nanyuki, Kenya – right on the equator. The ennui of camp life was deadening. 'People in prison camps do not live,' he later wrote. 'They only vegetate...' If only he could forget the past, he thought, then he would have no memory of joy, of freedom. That would be a blessing. Not that the present was any more bearable, where everybody got on each other's nerves at least some of the time. Some men were so bored that for hours they would crowd round the spectacle of a cat playing with a mouse.

The idea of escape was never far from Benuzzi's mind. But the nearest neutral territory – the Portuguese colony of Mozambique – was far to the south. Nearly a thousand miles (1,600 km) of British East Africa lay between him and freedom, a thousand miles of unknown terrain. He would need money, lots of money, a car, knowledge of the country, forged documents. During the five-year existence of Camp 354, many escaped with the intention of reaching Mozambique. Only four men succeeded.

> 'A gleaming snow-white peak with sparkling facets, which scintillated with the superb beauty of a colossal diamond.'

The Scottish explorer Joseph Thomson, in his book *Through Masai Land*, describes his first sight of Mount Kenya in 1883

Benuzzi was to hit upon an alternative ambition. He had arrived during the wet season, when the ground was a quagmire, the air thick with moisture, the sky reduced to a low ceiling of cloud, oppressing the spirits. Then early one morning in May a fellow prisoner came rushing into the hut, shaking Benuzzi awake. 'Quick. Get up,' he shouted, 'Come and look. Hurry, before the clouds close in again.' Benuzzi stumbled from his bunk to the door, and there, far to the southeast and high above a turbulent sea of clouds, there rose Africa's second highest peak – Mount Kenya. It was, Benuzzi recalled, 'a massive blue-black tooth of sheer rock inlaid with azure glaciers, austere yet floating fairy-like on the near horizon'. For some time afterwards, Benuzzi could barely speak. He was in love.

Birth of a dream

Benuzzi had acquired his love of mountains and mountaineering from his parents. He had begun his own climbing career on the great rock peaks of the Dolomites and the Julian Alps, but the war had brought an end to all that, had brought him to this place

PREVIOUS PAGE Felice Benuzzi: 'I was sure that everything we had endured, even the pain and hunger, would be sweet in memory.'

of the living dead. After that first vision the clouds closed in again, and it seemed to Benuzzi to have been a dream. Every time he looked in the direction in which he had seen the mountain, there was nothing. Then one night he saw it again, by starlight. And in a flash, he saw a way out of the dead-end in which his soul was lodged. He would plant a flag on that distant summit.

Mount Kenya, at over 17,000 feet (5,200 m), was the highest mountain he had ever laid eyes on. And it was no gentle snowy giant, but a great fang of rock. How would he adapt to the altitude? How, without ropes, pitons, karabiners, crampons and ice axes, would he overcome the obvious technical difficulties? Who – for it would be madness to climb alone – would join him? And how – before even attempting the ascent – would he manage to break out of the camp?

Benuzzi stopped smoking so he could use his cigarettes as currency in the camp, in order to acquire sufficient rations for the expedition, such as corned beef, jam, rice, sugar, biscuits, chocolate and sweets. Via the Red Cross, he asked his family back in Italy to send him his climbing boots and his warm woollen clothing, while a tailor in the camp made him a climbing suit out of blankets. The question of suitable companions was a tricky one, but a police lieutenant called Mario impressed him on account of his courage and enthusiasm. Although Mario had no mountaineering experience, he would make an ideal person to guard the base camp at the foot of the mountain.

> 'At the front one takes risks, but one does not suffer; in captivity one does not take risks but one suffers.'
>
> A First World War PoW, quoted by Benuzzi

ABOVE Mount Kenya from the southwest. The northwest ridge attempted by Benuzzi and his companion forms the left-hand skyline of the highest peak, Batian.

The equipment would have to be homemade, and to this end Benuzzi foraged for scrap metal in a rubbish dump, and managed to steal two hammers and a chisel from a store. A hammer became the basis of an ice axe, and metal from a car's running-board, bits of old mudguard and lengths of barbed wire were turned into crampons – sets of spikes to attach to one's boots, essential for climbing on the ice of glaciers.

One day someone produced a book by an Italian priest about the local people, the Kikuyu. The book contained some information about the mountain, a photograph, and a very small-scale map. Benuzzi found that a quiet fellow in his hut, a doctor called Giovanni Balletto – Giuàn to his friends – showed an interest in this book. After some discreet conversations, Benuzzi realized he had found an ideal climbing companion. The photograph in the book was taken from the east, from which side Mount Kenya's highest peak, Batian 17,058 feet (5,200 m) , threw down a great, impregnable wall of rock. A lower peak, Lenana 16,355 feet (4,985 m), appeared to be an easier climb, but Benuzzi had his heart set on Batian. They obtained a different view of the mountain from an unlikely source: the label on a tin of Kenylon meat and vegetables, manufactured by Oxo (South Africa) Ltd. This showed the mountain's southern aspect, from where it appeared equally formidable – and equally irresistible.

They waited for January, when the dry season would return, selecting the 24th as the day of their escape. But on New Year's Day they learnt that Mario was to be transferred to another camp. Recovering from this set-back, Benuzzi and Giuàn soon put out feelers to recruit a replacement. After a couple of disappointments, Giuàn suggested an old friend of his called Enzo Barsotti. He was unfit, a heavy smoker, and 'universally thought to be as mad as a hatter'. A madman – particularly such an amiable, enthusiastic madman – was, they decided, precisely what they needed for their harebrained adventure. Only a madman would contemplate with equanimity the perils in store – the armed patrols, the forests, the wild animals, the blizzards, the sheer cliffs – only to return to captivity. For this too was part of the plan; there was nowhere else for them to go. With only a week left before the planned escape, they had no hesitation in asking Enzo to join them.

THE NAMES OF MOUNT KENYA

THE KIKUYU NAME FOR MOUNT KENYA IS KERE-NYAGA, meaning 'mountain of brightness'. The Wakamba version of this name is Kenyaa, the basis of the European name. The Masai call the mountain Ol-Donyo-Eibor, 'the white mountain', and the highest point, Batian, was named by Sir Halford Mackinder, the leader of the first ascent in 1899, in honour of a historical Masai medicine man called Mbatian. Two of the lower peaks, Nelion and Lenana, were named by Mackinder after two of Mbatian's sons. The col between Batian and Nelion is the Gate of the Mists, and below this plunges the line of ice known as the Diamond Couloir.

Above the abodes of men

Escape was remarkably easy. Security was much slacker in African PoW camps than in Europe, because no one expected the prisoners to bother to escape – and any escapee would stand out like a sore thumb among the native population, if they weren't first eaten by lions. The prisoners at Camp 354 were allowed to cultivate their own vegetables outside the compound, and sometimes were permitted to unlock the gate themselves. Among the rows of vegetables in the gardens the three would-be escapees concealed all their food and equipment – which also now included ropes, a tent made out of groundsheets, blankets, a large aluminium water bottle, an improvised alcohol stove with fuel 'acquired' from the camp hospital, solidified mutton fat for waterproofing their boots, torches, a panga for slashing a path through the forest, and a host of other bits and pieces – most crucially, a compass. For the actual escape from the camp, Benuzzi managed to make a copy of the key to the gate of the compound. At midday on Sunday 24 January, while the British officers were at lunch, he unlocked the gate. The African guard simply assumed that he and his companions were going to work in the gardens. It looked like the long months of preparation were going to pay off.

They rested in the gardens till nightfall, then, burdened under enormous rucksacks, made their way across the thorn scrub and grassland, aiming to cross the railway and the main road before moonrise. In a few hours they had passed these barriers, and traversed the last of the farmland where their presence might have raised the alarm. Sometime after midnight they reached the relative safety of the forest. This safety was indeed only relative, for the forest was home to dangerous animals such as rhinoceros, elephant, leopard, lion and, most to be feared, buffalo. Once hidden among the trees, they settled down to sleep as day broke. And so they continued, travelling along tracks through the forest by the light of the stars at night, resting during the day, while one man kept watch for people – or wild beasts. The noises of the forest at night sent shivers down their spines. Aiming to conserve their supplies, they restricted their daily intake per man to one hard-boiled egg, two small biscuits and a third of a tin of corned beef.

Eventually they came to a river in a steep-sided valley. Although it was the dry season, the river was full, a sure sign that it was being fed by the glaciers of the great mountain hidden somewhere above them. It was hard work following the river, jumping from rock to rock or scrambling up the craggy banks to cut a trail through the thick undergrowth. But at least now, as they rose above the abodes of men, they could travel by daylight.

> '
> Sir,
> We have not previously informed you of our intentions, sure that you would try to dissuade us. We are leaving the camp and reckon to be back within fourteen days. Then you will know and certainly approve of our action ...
> '

Letter left by Benuzzi and his companions for the Italian liaison officer at the camp

Although they were on the equator, with increasing altitude the nights brought a damp cold that penetrated to their bones. And yet, despite their discomforts and their heavy loads, they were buoyed up by their temporary liberty, enthralled by the beauties and marvels of nature, as the splendour of the tropical forest, interspersed with thickets of bamboo, gave way at about 10,000 feet (3,000 m) to a zone of huge heathers draped in lichen, and then, higher still, a surreal landscape of mosses and swamps, giant groundsels and lobelias. There were moments of tension – including close encounters in the forest with a leopard, a rhino and a bull-elephant. In this last instance, the magnificence of the animal inspired more wonder than terror. 'He was worth everything,' one of them remarked after the elephant retreated back into the trees, 'all our past and future toils.'

No success like failure

It was eight days after walking out of Camp 354 that they got their first close-up look at their objective: 'There it was at last, our ultimate goal, its appalling north face armoured with ice, its jagged pinnacles not yet touched by the rising sun, dreamlike, overwhelming ...' At 14,000 feet (4,300 m) they were feeling the effects of the altitude. Both Enzo and Giuàn had suffered fevers on the approach march, and now Enzo, after over-exerting himself, had actually passed out, his heart threatening to fail. He had to be revived with some strong coffee dripped between his lips. They had intended establishing their base camp higher, nearer to the mountain, but Giuàn, the doctor, declared that Enzo, their base-camp guardian, must not go a step further.

Benuzzi and Giuàn had no information about the mountain itself, beyond the picture on the Kenylon label. They did not know it, but the route they were going to attempt, the northwest ridge, had first been climbed in 1930 by Eric Shipton and H.W. Tilman, two of the leading British climbers of the interwar period, who both went on to distinguish themselves on Everest. Shipton and Tilman had made their ascent in August, which is summer on the north side of the mountain, and the rocks were free from snow – but still it was a formidable climb, and had yet to have a second ascent. Now it was February. And they were nearly out of food.

A day reconnoitring the route ahead was followed by a day of rest and preparation. At 3 a.m. on 4 February, having breakfasted on two biscuits apiece, washed down with sweetened Ovaltine prepared for them by Enzo, Benuzzi and Giuàn began their attempt. The ground was frozen, and reaching a col they were greeted by an icy blast. Dawn broke just as they reached the beginning of the real climbing. Above them the sky was a shade of deep blue-violet; below them, the plains and

> Above all our outing had been a reaction against the sluggish life of a PoW camp, an act of will amidst all that inertia.

Felice Benuzzi, *No Picnic on Mount Kenya* (1953)

foothills were hidden beneath a sea of cloud, across which stretched out the shadow of the great mountain itself. At first, all went well: the rock was sound, their homemade ice axes dealt successfully with the passages of hard ice they encountered. Only their sisal rope – previously used in the camp to tie bedding-nets to bunks and so thin that they climbed with it doubled – gave them cause for anxiety.

> ... it occurs to me that, from one point of view, ours was a conceited and even mad venture.
>
> Felice Benuzzi, *No Picnic on Mount Kenya* (1953)

After crossing a series of cols and subsidiary ridges, at 11 a.m. they reached the foot of the northeast ridge itself. At first it was easy, but as they climbed higher the rocks became smoother and smoother, and increasingly they were covered in snow. A little after midday mists began to snake around the ridge, the wind increased, and a snowstorm was upon them. Giuàn, who was in the lead, shouted down that he could see no possibility of going any further. He wasn't even sure if he could get back down to his companion. They held a short conversation, yelling in the teeth of the blast. Their conclusion was that retreat was the only option. It took Giuàn 40 minutes to climb down to Benuzzi, through snow and hail. As they continued the perilous descent, their clothes became rigid with ice, and their frozen fingers could barely grasp the rock. Their exhaustion – after days of hard labour on inadequate rations, and nights deprived of sleep – began to tell. The thick mist and the new snow made their route upward almost unrecognizable. All this meant that they had to redouble the care they took at every downward step.

At last, after 12 hours of rock climbing, they reached easier ground. They consoled themselves that they had given it their best shot; staying alive is always a kind of victory on a mountain. And they had their second objective still to try – Lenana. But for now, the descent was all they could think of, the interminable descent. As darkness fell they still had not reached the camp where Enzo waited for them. Their exhaustion brought them to the brink of despair: Benuzzi began to hallucinate, Giuàn let out the occasional sob. But they never gave up, and in the end, out of the murk, the beam of their torch caught the shape of the tent. It was almost nine o'clock; they had been on the go for 18 hours.

After a day's rest, they made a successful ascent of Lenana, a lower, easier peak than Batian, but – exceeding as it does the height of Mont Blanc – a considerable achievement in their condition. On the summit they left their names in a bottle and hoisted the flag of the Kingdom of Italy. They were content with their climb. And yet, looking across to Batian, rising high and impregnable above them,

> We comforted ourselves with the thought that our eyes had feasted on unforgettable scenes to compensate us for what our mouths had lacked.
>
> Felice Benuzzi, *No Picnic on Mount Kenya* (1953)

they did experience, as any true climber would, a shiver of regret. Once they returned to base camp, Benuzzi ruefully remembered, they celebrated by missing out on dinner.

The mountain remains

It was with some sadness that they left base camp the following day. But, with virtually no food left – less than half a pound of rice, some tea and coffee, and one biscuit each – it was their intention to get back behind barbed wire as soon as they possibly could. They had taken nine days on the way up; their aim was to descend in three.

They could think and talk of nothing but food. Although they had abandoned much of their gear, their rucksacks seemed as heavy as they had on the way up. 'I felt weary beyond belief,' Benuzzi recalled, 'yet I was sure that everything we had endured, even the pain and hunger ... would be sweet in memory.' They slipped and slithered down the slopes, down through the forest, cut by thorns and stung by giant nettles, letting out Tarzan yells to keep up their spirits.

By the third day, black shadows were dancing in front of Benuzzi's eyes. There was a constant humming in his ears, his balance began to fail, and fall followed fall as he stumbled back down the rocky river bed. The others were in no better shape. Bitter wild olives failed to relieve their hunger. Apathy began to creep up on them, but neither their sense of fun nor their determination ever quite deserted them. On they marched, into the night, until they could go no further and lay down to sleep.

OVER THE HIMALAYA

HEINRICH HARRER, FAMOUS AS THE AUTHOR OF *SEVEN YEARS IN TIBET*, was another mountaineer interned by the British during the Second World War. He had achieved considerable fame after his first ascent of the notoriously dangerous North Wall of the Eiger in 1938, and the following year joined a small German expedition intent on reconnoitring a new route up Nanga Parbat, one of the most perilous of the Himalayan giants. One day in early September they were waiting in Karachi, in what was then British India, for a ship to take them back to Germany, sipping cool beer in a hotel garden with the friendly local police chief, when a squad of soldiers came to arrest them. War had broken out in Europe. Eventually Harrer found himself in an internment camp in Dehra Dun, in the foothills of the Himalaya in northern India. Security was not tight – civilian internees were given passes to leave the camp – and Harrer absconded on a number of occasions, but each time he was recaptured. At last, in May 1944, he and his fellow-mountaineer Peter Aufschnaiter were successful, crossing a pass nearly 20,000 feet (16,000 m) high to enter Tibet, then largely barred to outsiders. After further adventures he reached Lhasa, where he began his long association with the Dalai Lama.

Shortly after midnight they resumed their weary way. At every stumble and fall, it was a temptation to sleep once more, but the longer they delayed, the longer they would be without food. At last they came to their vegetable gardens just outside the camp, but the food they'd hoped to find there was missing. Now at last, though, they could sleep.

In the morning, they mingled with the other prisoners working in the vegetable gardens, and thus smuggled themselves back into the camp. Benuzzi, Giuàn and Enzo were once more Prisoners of War 762, 41303 and 41304. They were sentenced, as expected, to 28 days in the cells, but they did not mind their confinement. They had food and water, and their friends smuggled them books and cigarettes. Above all, they had a view through the bars of the window of the object of all their dreams and efforts: the 'colossal diamond' of Mount Kenya. After seven days, the camp commandant, who appreciated their 'sporting effort', released them from the cells.

It was not until August 1946 that Benuzzi was repatriated. He went on to publish a best-selling – and beautifully written – account of his wartime adventure, *No Picnic on Mount Kenya*, and pursued a career in the Italian diplomatic service, eventually attaining the rank of ambassador. He continued to climb wherever he went. In 1974, nearing retirement, he paid a return visit to the mountain that meant so much to him. 'The Mountain has accompanied us throughout our lives,' his wife Stefania commented, 'Wherever we were, Mount Kenya was there too.'

Felice Benuzzi died in 1988.

> So hungry for adventure and hazard were we ... that joyfully and happily we went on into the forest towards the lonely equatorial peaks, into a world untainted by man's misery and bright with promise.

Felice Benuzzi, *No Picnic on Mount Kenya* (1953)

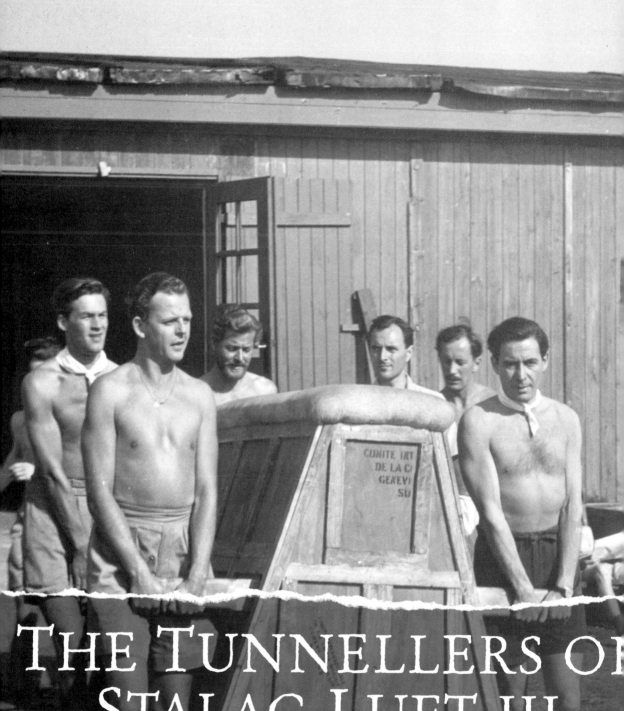

The Tunnellers of Stalag Luft III

The stories behind *The Wooden Horse* and *The Great Escape*, 1943–

Stalag Luft III, run by the Luftwaffe as a prison for captured Allied airmen, was intended to be tunnel-proof. And yet the camp – which at one point held over 10,000 prisoners – was to see two of the most famous tunnelling escapes of the Second World War. One of these attempts was to end in triumph, the other in tragedy. Both inspired books by former prisoners – *The Wooden Horse* by Eric Williams and *The Great Escape* by Paul Brickhill – and these in turn gave rise to famous feature films: that of *The Great Escape* in particular, although substantially fictionalized, has become a cornerstone of popular culture.

The site of Stalag Luft III – a hundred miles southeast of Berlin near Sagan, Silesia (now Zagan in Poland) – was chosen because of the sandy subsoil, which meant that any tunnel would be liable to collapse. Furthermore, excavated sand, when still damp, was bright yellow, and then dried to a brilliant whiteness; either wet or dry, it would contrast with the grey dust of the surface and betray the fact that digging was in progress. To make matters even more difficult, the barracks were positioned far from the perimeter fence and raised on piles three feet (1 m) above the ground, making it difficult to conceal any tunnelling activity. Finally, seismographic microphones were strategically placed around the camp, so that the noise of any digging could be detected.

The Wooden Horse

On the outbreak of war Eric Williams had abandoned a career in a Liverpool department store to volunteer for the RAF. After training in Canada as a navigator and bomb-aimer, he joined a bomber squadron – No. 75 (New Zealand) – based near Cambridge. Life expectancy for bomber crews at that time was about a dozen missions at most, so in some ways Flight Lieutenant Williams was lucky when he managed to bail out of his shot-up Stirling bomber during a raid on the Ruhr on 17 December 1942. It was the end of a tragic year for Williams: his wife Joan had died during a German air raid on Liverpool, and two of his three brothers had been killed while serving with the RAF. Now he was a prisoner of war. His mother was informed that he was missing, presumed dead.

When Williams arrived at Stalag Luft III, it was the midst of winter, and the season partly disguised the harsh realities of camp life:

> Snow lay thickly on the roofs of the barrack blocks and gave an air of gaiety to the barbed wire which sparkled and glittered in the sun. Every post carried its cap of crisp, powdery snow, and when the wind blew, the snow drifted up against the coiled wire, softening its gauntness.

OPPOSITE A still from the feature film *The Wooden Horse* showing British PoWs bringing out the vaulting horse they used to disguise their tunnelling operation.

'All the compounds were surrounded by two parallel-running fences, three metres high, about two metres apart, and tightly strung with barbed wire. The space between the fences was filled up with coiled and tangled barbed wire, about one metre high. This was called the '*Lowengang*' ('Lion's Walk'). In the actual compounds, about ten metres from the inside barbed-wire fence, were affixed small stakes with wire, circling the compound. This marked the so-called 'warning line'. The crossing of this line was expressly forbidden ...'

Friedrich-Wilhelm von Lindeiner-Wildau, commandant of Stalag Luft III, 1942–4, quoted in Charles Rollings, *Prisoner of War: Voices from Captivity during the Second World War* (2007)

The men used their bed-boards as toboggans, and flooded the football pitch to make an ice rink. There was something of a holiday atmosphere.

But with the return of spring, Williams turned his mind to thoughts of escape, and with another prisoner, Lieutenant Michael Codner of the Royal Artillery, he hatched an ingenious plan. Earlier tunnelling attempts from underneath the barracks had been easily spotted by the guards, so Williams audaciously proposed to start his tunnel in the open, much nearer to the perimeter fence. To disguise what was going on, he and Codner constructed a vaulting horse out of plywood from Red Cross parcels, and persuaded other prisoners to start using it for exercise in the open air, as near to the wire as they could. Each day the horse was carried out to the same spot, with a man hidden inside. Once the horse was in position, and the gymnasts started their noisy jumps, the man would start his digging. The noise of the gymnastics, as well as providing a visual distraction, masked the noise of tunnelling from the seismographic microphones.

Eventually, Williams and Codner were joined by a third man, Flight Lieutenant Oliver Philpot. Over a period of four and a half months, using bowls for shovels and metal rods to poke holes up to the surface for air, they created a tunnel more than 100 feet (30 m) long. On the evening of 29 October 1943 the three men emerged out of the far end, beyond the wire. This was just the beginning of their adventures. As they made their way across Germany, their clothing and forged travel documents became more and more frayed, and they were in a constant state of anxiety that they would make some slip that would betray them. Williams and Codner, disguised as French workmen, eventually reached the Baltic port of Stettin (now Szczecin in Poland). Here they stowed away on a ship bound for Denmark, from where they made their way to neutral Sweden. Philpot, in the guise of a Norwegian margarine salesman, took a train to Danzig (now Gdansk), where he smuggled himself onto a Swedish ship bound for Göteborg. All three eventually found their way back to Britain, where in 1944 they were each awarded the Military Cross.

Tom, Dick and Harry

The escape of Williams and his two companions was a small-scale affair compared to that envisaged by the head of the escape committee, Squadron Leader Roger Bushell – known as 'Big X'. It was Bushell (renamed Roger Barlett and played by Richard Attenborough in the film of *The Great Escape*) who organized and led the project by which three tunnels were to be dug under the wire, with the aim of liberating some two hundred men – not so much with the expectation that they would all find their way home, but with the intention of causing the maximum disruption to the German war effort. The aim was, according to Bushell, to 'harass, confuse and confound the enemy'. Bushell, a single-minded character, was very security conscious, and threatened any man who even mentioned the word 'tunnel' with a court martial. Instead, the three tunnels were named Tom, Dick and Harry.

The starting points of the three tunnels were carefully selected. The entrance to Tom was in the dark corner of a hall, Dick began in the drain sump of a shower room, and Harry started under a stove. The tunnels – about 2 feet (60 cm) square – were dug some 30 feet (9 m) down, so that the noise would not be picked up by the microphones. Bed boards were used to shore up the sandy walls, tins were bent into shape for use as digging tools, animal fat was skimmed off the top of soup to provide fuel for lamps. Squadron Leader Bob Nelson improvised an air pump, by which much needed oxygen was delivered to the diggers via pipes made out of tins. A small-scale railway was laid along the tunnels, and the excavators ferried themselves to the 'coal face' lying on trucks. Much of the tunnelling work relied on the expertise of Flight Lieutenant Wally Floody of the Royal Canadian Air Force, who had worked as a miner before the war (and who was the inspiration behind Flight Lieutenant Danny Velinski, 'the Tunnel King', the character played by Charles Bronson in the film). Floody was transferred to another camp before the breakout. In charge of forging documents for the escapees was Group Captain Nicolas Tindal-Carill-Worsley. Prior to the breakout he offered his place to a fellow officer whose wife was expecting a baby back in England.

Work on Dick was abandoned after the Germans cleared the forest where it was intended to surface. Thereafter Dick was used for storage, and to hide excavated sand from the

> ‘He could describe the damp barrack blocks, fetid and close from overcrowded living, the rows and rows of two-tier bunks, the scuffing of wooden clogs on damp concrete as the bearded and dirty kriegies [PoWs] queued up for the midday ration of cabbage water ... But what could he say of the companionship ... What could he say of the decency and humour of the average man. Words could not convey what he felt ...’
>
> Eric Williams, *The Wooden Horse* (1949)

> I was stuck once, at Leicester Square, one of the halfway houses in the tunnel, and I've never been so terrified in my life. I was sweating with fear. I was pulled out after 30 minutes but it seemed like a year.

Anthony Bethell, one of the tunnellers who survived the break-out, quoted in Tim Carroll, *The Great Escapers* (2004)

other tunnels. Prior to this the men had put the sand in old socks concealed in their trousers, scattering it through a small hole as they walked around the camp. Alternatively, they dumped it in the gardens they were allowed to cultivate – but in due course the guards (known as 'ferrets' or 'goons') became too suspicious. After Dick was abandoned, work on the other two tunnels intensified, but soon the Germans discovered the entrance to Tom. Only Harry was left. It was finally completed in March 1944.

Quite a number of US servicemen had been involved in the construction of the tunnels, but before Harry was completed they were transferred to a different compound – and so, despite what the film would have us believe, no Americans were involved in the actual breakout. It was lucky for them that they weren't.

Hitler's savage retribution

The date set for the breakout was the first moonless night after Harry was completed: Friday 24 March. That night the hut was so jam-packed with would-be escapers, all dressed in heavy coats, that steam billowed out the windows. But the guards didn't notice. Excitement turned to tension which in turn gave way to frustration as the men waited hours for their turn. When it was time to go, some who had not been involved in the excavation work found it claustrophobic in the tunnel, and there was the occasional shimmer of panic. When the first man emerged from the far end he found to his alarm that the exit was just short of the trees. Nevertheless, 75 men followed him out. Then, at 5 a.m. in the morning, the 77th man was spotted by a guard, and the alarm was raised.

With snow lying on the ground, the escaped prisoners were forced to stick to the roads, and it was not long before the vast majority were rounded up. In fact, only three men achieved 'home runs': the Norwegians Per Bergsland and Jens Müller, who made it to Sweden, and the Dutchman Bram van der Stok, who made his way through France to neutral Spain.

> When I got to the exit shaft I climbed up the ladder and the first thing I saw were stars. I thought of the RAF motto – *Per Ardua ad Astra* – "through adversity to the stars."

Bertram 'Jimmy' James, MC, quoted in Tim Carroll, *The Great Escapers* (2004)

The Nazis were concerned that escaped Allied PoWs were fomenting unrest among the millions of foreign workers forced to labour in Germany. Hitler was incandescent with rage when he heard of the escape. He wanted all 73 men who had been recaptured to be shot as a warning to others, but the

German High Command were worried about retaliations on German PoWs in Britain. In the end a compromise was agreed: 50 men – 22 Britons, 6 Canadians, 6 Poles, 4 Australians, 3 South Africans, 2 New Zealanders, 2 Norwegians, a Belgian, a Czech, a Frenchman, a Greek and a Lithuanian – were taken off by the Gestapo in small groups to remote locations, where they were shot through the back of the head. Among those murdered were Squadron Leader Roger Bushell, and the expectant father for whom Nicolas Tindal-Carill-Worsley had given up his place.

One of the female German mail-censors at Stalag Luft III remembered the grim atmosphere when she returned to the camp after the executions: 'There was deep mourning and grieving about the shot ones, especially with those censors who had lost one of their "customers".' When he heard what had happened, Hauptmann Hans Pieber, a German officer on the camp staff, told the PoWs: 'I hope not one of you Englishmen will even think that the Luftwaffe had anything to do with this terrible deed.'

After the war, the killers were tracked down and brought to justice. Fourteen were hanged, and several others received heavy prison sentences. Johannes Post, one

ABOVE Eighteen members of the Gestapo were put on trial in Hamburg in 1947, charged with the murder of 50 of the Great Escapers. All but four of the accused were hanged.

THE ORIGINAL COOLER KING

IN REALITY, NO AMERICANS WERE INVOLVED IN THE ACTUAL BREAKOUT through the Harry tunnel, but in the film one of the more prominent escapers is Captain Virgil Hilts, played by Steve McQueen. Hilts is nicknamed the Cooler King owing to the number of times he has tried to escape, resulting in spells in the 'cooler' – the punishment cells. Hilts was partly based on a US pilot called Alvin Vogtle, who made five escape attempts from various camps, and on the sixth attempt, in March 1945, made it to Switzerland. Other aspects of the character were inspired by Squadron Leader Eric Foster of the RAF.

Foster was shot down in June 1940, the only survivor of an eight-man crew, sustaining two broken legs when his parachute failed to open properly. While still convalescing, he attempted to escape by climbing down a drainpipe. Recaptured, he was sent to the notorious castle-prison of Colditz, but walked out again wearing a stolen Hitler Youth uniform. He got as far as the Swiss border. His next camp was Schubin in Poland, where conditions were appalling, and escape was a matter of survival. After eight months digging, the tunnel system he and his fellow officers were working on was detected by the guards. His last camp was Stalag Luft III. Here he was not involved in the tunnelling operation, but came up with an alternative ruse. By studying medical textbooks in the camp library, he learned to feign the symptoms of mental illness so effectively that he was repatriated on health grounds. The trouble was, once back in Britain, he found himself confined to a mental institution, and experienced some difficulty convincing the medical authorities that he was, in fact, quite sane. Subsequently, if he found himself in an argument, he would put the following question to his interlocutor: 'I can prove I'm not mad – can you?' Eric Foster died in 2006 at the age of 102.

of those executed, had no regrets. He said the Allied airmen were *Terrorfliegers*, terror fliers, subhumans who deserved to die. Another of the killers, Alfred Schimmel, was a devout Christian and could not bring himself to carry out his orders to shoot his victim on Good Friday. So he shot him on Thursday instead.

The survivors

In 1994, 50 years after the breakout, services were held at the memorial to the murdered men at Zagan, and at the site of their final resting place in the Polish city of Poznan. One of the former inmates of Stalag Luft III who made the pilgrimage was Flight Lieutenant Lionel Jeffries of the Royal Australian Air Force. 'The camp,' he reported, 'is no more ...'

> ... no huts, no barbed wire and no guard towers. The area is now a young,
> sparse forest. But down on the forest floor remain important traces of the
> camp's existence. In particular, a depression in the well-remembered sandy
> loam, in which lies a slab of concrete lying at a drunken angle ... The slab was

the base of a stove which concealed the opening to the tunnel ...

The memorial, erected in 1944 by the camp inmates themselves with the permission of the guilt-ridden commandant, is in a fenced-off area of the forest. During the service, Jeffries recalled, 'The cold wind blowing could not be entirely blamed for so many watery eyes.'

In 2004, for his book *The Great Escapers*, Tim Carroll interviewed the handful of men from the breakout who were still alive. 'Was it worth it?' Flight Lieutenant Les Brodrick asked himself. 'Fifty men dead, and only a few months before the end of the war? No, it wasn't worth it.' Flight Lieutenant Sydney Dowse, MC, disagreed. After his recapture he was sent to Sachsenhausen, but escaped again. 'The Great Escape was worth it,' he said. 'We caused havoc to the Germans.' Flight Lieutenant Dick Churchill, another of those interviewed, said: 'I'd rather not dwell on what happened nearly sixty years ago. I'd rather concentrate on what my five grandchildren are going to do in their lives.' Pilot Officer Paul Royle, of the Royal Australian Air Force, shrugged the whole thing off: 'It never seemed so important to those who took part in it as it does to others. There were millions of people doing all sorts of things in that war and we were just a small part of it.'

'+++ IN VIEW OF INCREASING GERMAN RUTHLESSNESS AND LACK OF REGARD TO GENEVA CONVENTION CHIEFS OF STAFF RULE THAT UNDER PRESENT CIRCUMSTANCES IT NEED NO LONGER BE CONSIDERED DUTY OF P/W TO ESCAPE BUT IT IS NOT FORBIDDEN TO DO SO. DO NOT LET GERMANS KNOW. +++++'

Message from IS9 (Intelligence School No. 9) to the senior British officer at Stalag Luft III, in the aftermath of the mass executions

EVADING THE ENEMY

A US airman avoids capture in occupied France, 1943–4

During the Second World War, some quarter of a million US, British and Commonwealth servicemen were held prisoner by the Germans. A handful managed to escape from the camps, which were mostly situated in eastern Germany or Poland, but only a small number made it the long way back home. But there were also thousands of Allied airmen – perhaps as many as 5,000 – who were shot down over Nazi-occupied territory in France, Belgium and Holland, who, with the help of escape lines organized by the Resistance, evaded capture altogether, and found their way back to Britain to fly and fight another day. This is the story of just one of them, First Lieutenant (later Lieutenant Colonel) James ('Jim') E. Armstrong, a B-17 pilot of the US Eighth Air Force, who spent five months on the run in France before making it back to Britain and freedom.

Aircrews knew the attrition rate from bombing raids over Germany was appalling: over 55,000 men from RAF Bomber Command, 44 per cent of those who flew, lost their lives. The US Eighth Air Force suffered a further 26,000 men killed, and, on average, 1 in 20 planes failed to return from any single mission. 'Since we had to fly 25 missions before rotating back to the States,' Bombardier Ed Burley recalled, 'it didn't take a mathematical wizard to work out that statistically it would be impossible to finish a tour of duty without being shot down.'

The possibility that they could get home if they were shot down and had to bail out of a burning aircraft over enemy-occupied territory was a significant morale booster, and as part of their training aircrews were taught how to make contact with sympathetic locals, and how to live off the land if need be. Both the British and the Americans had small departments dedicated to helping evaders, MI9 and MIS-X respectively, but their work in returning highly trained men to action was never as appreciated as much as it should have been. Also largely overlooked was the covert work of innumerable French, Belgian and Dutch civilians who expressed their detestation of their Nazi occupiers by helping Allied airmen to safety, in the full knowledge that if they were caught they would be shot.

> 'It didn't take a mathematical wizard to work out that statistically it would be impossible to finish a tour of duty without being shot down.'
>
> Bombardier Ed Burley, 331st Bomb Squadron, US Eighth Air Force

OPPOSITE An American B-17 'Flying Fortress' over Berlin, February 1945. Perhaps as many as 5,000 Allied airmen shot down over Nazi-occupied Europe managed to evade capture and make it back to Britain.

Training for survival

The first thing the would-be evader had to learn was how to escape from a shot-up bomber. Parachute training was rudimentary – sometimes no more than a jump from a platform or tethered balloon, or a roll from the back of a slow-moving truck. There was also some basic instruction on how to make an emergency exit, but in the training exercises the aeroplane was always horizontal, stationary and earthbound. So none of this really prepared a flier for the nightmare of finding himself in a burning aircraft in a nosedive or vertical tailspin, fighting against the G-force, the cold and the flames, desperately trying to reach the escape hatch and then struggling to open it and get out without snagging straps or buckles or radio headsets. Thousands never made it.

But for those who did, it was only the beginning. The roar and panic and screams were left behind, and suddenly the flier was alone in the cold silence of space, floating slowly down towards the earth. On landing, aircrew were told to hide the parachute, and to move quickly away. They were also advised to empty their bladders and bowels, giving them an opportunity to calm down, gather their thoughts and make a plan. Some found this good advice, but other suggestions were bizarrely unhelpful. One squadron was briefed by an intelligence officer that in France it was acceptable to sleep with a man's wife, or his daughter, but if you made off with his bicycle you would wake up with your throat cut. Some were told to avoid making contact with French priests, as the Catholic Church was a bastion of right-wing Nazi sympathizers, while others were told that priests, along with teachers and farmers, were a good bet. This conflicting advice was not surprising, given that France was split between those who deeply resented the German occupiers and those who actively collaborated with them.

'We never talked about the possibilities of being shot down or being an evader. It was something you told yourself just wouldn't happen to you.'

Pilot Officer George Fernyhough, of the RAF, who was shot down over the Netherlands

In addition to such advice, aircrew were also provided with 'escape aids', many of them devised by the eccentric Lieutenant Christopher Clayton Hutton, MI9's technical officer and a fan of Harry Houdini (see box, page 108). The most important items were maps, printed on thin silk, and a compass, disguised as a button or collar stud or hidden in a pipe or a pen. Then there were bootlaces made of serrated wire for use as a saw, and flying boots that could be cut down to look like civilian shoes, and with hollow heels for hiding useful items. Essential for survival during the first 48 hours on the ground, before the downed airman could make contact with local sympathizers, was the 'escape kit', a flat tin that contained sweets, chocolate, amphetamines, water-purifying tablets, a razor, a needle and thread, a rubber water carrier, matches and 50 cigarettes. One of the most difficult things to get right were forged documents, as civilians in occupied countries could be stopped at any time and asked to produce their papers – not only an ID card, but also a work permit, ration card, demobilization papers, and so on. The regulations were always changing, and Allied intelligence did not always keep up, so many evaders ended up being caught out with the wrong, or out-of-date, documents.

Shot down over Normandy

When First Lieutenant Jim Armstrong started flying B-17 Flying Fortresses in tight formation over Europe, his unit, the 384th Bombardment Group, US Eighth Air Force, was losing a hundred men a month. It did not take him long to figure that it was only sensible to be prepared for the worst, and so always carried with him the sheet of French phrases that he had been issued with. He couldn't pronounce the words, but he could point. The first phrase read: '*Je suis un aviateur américain.*'

In September 1943, just a month after his 21st birthday, he took off on what turned out to be his last mission – his 11th. The target was the VKF ball-bearing plant in Stuttgart. On the return, his B-17 was slowed down by headwinds, and by a hit from anti-aircraft fire in one of the engines. Then, over France, a German Focke-Wulf Fw 190 attacked, damaging a wing, and, on a return pass, set the B-17 on fire with a hit from its 20 mm cannons. The crew bailed out and landed near the village of Étrépagny, not far from Rouen in Normandy. Although one of the crew was killed, Armstrong sustained no more than a sprained ankle and bruises, together with burns to his face and hands.

Soon after landing, as he was drinking water from a ditch, Armstrong was accosted by a Frenchman, a veteran of the First World War, who told him to hide in the woods, and for over a week brought him food twice a day, until his neighbours grew suspicious. Using a compass disguised as a pocket watch, Armstrong set off on foot along the banks of the River Seine, which he knew would eventually take him to Paris. There he hoped to make contact with the Resistance. After two days he reached the village of Triel-sur-Seine, just to the west of the capital, where a doctor took him in, treated his burns, and took him by train to his apartment in Paris. Here Armstrong was picked up by members of the Resistance, who took him to the suburb of Drancy – infamous as the site of an internment centre where French Jews were held prior to deportation to the death camps in the east (see page 115).

> 'The good escaper is the man who keeps himself fit, cheerful and comfortable. He is not a 'he-man' who boasts about his capacity to endure discomfort. He should be a man with sound common sense and above all a man of great determination.'
>
> *Tips for Evaders and Escapers*, issued by MI9, July 1944

Fourth time lucky

In Drancy Armstrong met up with two fellow Americans and an Englishmen, and he and the others were issued with false IDs. Armstrong's alias was Jean Riber, a butcher. They were sent back west, to the port of Quimper in Brittany, for the first of several escape attempts. The plan, organized by Yves Le Hénaff, who had set up the 'Dahlia' Circuit in Quimper, was for Armstrong and nine other Allied airmen to be taken out to sea in a fishing boat to rendezvous with a British MTB (motor torpedo boat). But before this could happen their safe house was visited by the French police, working for the Vichy collaborationist regime, and Armstrong and the others had to escape out of a back window and make a dash for another refuge. Then news came that the owner of the dock where the fishing boat was moored had been told by his wife not to have anything to do with the escapade. Before other arrangements could be made, the deadline of 1 November for making the rendezvous with the MTB had been missed.

Armstrong and his companions were returned to Paris, while a new escape plan was hatched. It was always dangerous travelling by train with forged documents, but they managed to avoid close scrutiny. Then, in mid-December they went south, with the aim of traversing the mountain barrier of the Pyrenees and reaching neutral

ABOVE Members of the French Resistance in central France receive a consignment of air-dropped weapons, August 1944. As well as actively fighting the Germans, the Resistance helped many Allied servicemen to escape.

Spain. Arriving in the medieval walled town of Carcassone, Armstrong was alarmed to see German soldiers checking the papers of the passengers. 'The game's up,' he thought. 'One look at my false ID card, a few questions and I'm on my way to a PoW camp. There's no escape.' But there was. Their resourceful guide ushered them into the public lavatory on the platform, where they spent a cold and anxious hour. When they re-emerged, the Germans had gone. But there was deep snow on the ground, and it was clear that attempting a crossing of the Pyrenees in these conditions would be foolhardy – a conclusion presumably shared by the man who was to guide them over the mountains, as he failed to turn up. On the way back to Paris their guide kept them safe from the attentions of the Germans on the train by moving them from carriage to carriage.

On Christmas Day Armstrong found himself back in Brittany, at the fishing harbour of Tréboul, northwest of Quimper. That night, he and about 30 others waded out to a waiting boat, only to be told that the mission was off – the store of diesel on board had been locked up, no one had the key, and the lock could not be broken without the noise alerting the patrolling Germans. So back they went to their various safe houses.

> It is possible that your bowels will not move regularly if you are living on strict Escape Box rations. Do not let this alarm you.
>
> *Tips for Evaders and Escapers*, issued by MI9, July 1944

'REMEMBER EVERYTHING BUT WRITE NOTHING'

THIS WAS THE STERN WARNING to prospective evaders given in a briefing document issued by MI9. It continued:

> One address on a scrap of paper can result in the tracing of many helpers. Never discuss your previous helpers with those with whom you find yourself next. Security must be of the highest order. There have been cases where evaders and escapers have sent postcards back to helpers thanking them. The motive may be good but the supreme stupidity of their actions is almost incredible. Do nothing which can endanger your helpers' lives. They do what they do without thought of reward. All they ask is that you do not talk. They trust their lives to your hands. Do not betray that trust.

Even when they got home, evaders were told to keep quiet about their adventures – what routes they had taken, who had helped them. One returnee, ignoring this, gave a friend and fellow flier a note of the name and address of a French farmer and his wife who had looked after him. The friend put the note in his wallet. When, several months later, this man was shot down and taken prisoner by the Germans, the note was found. The farmer and his wife were shot.

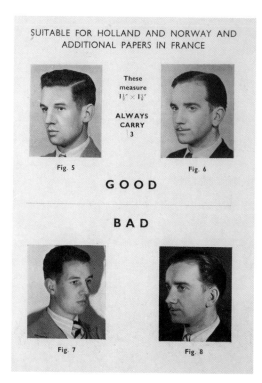

ABOVE Extracts from a leaflet issued to RAF crews showing the types of photograph they should carry with them for use in false ID papers. These examples of 'good' and 'bad' photographs were accompanied by various 'points to watch'. For instance, the caption to Fig. 3 advises: 'Try not to look as if you are "Wanted". Also avoid the smiling picture as in Fig. 4. 'Subjects must look tidy but not ultra smart.' Regarding Fig. 4: 'Open collars must not be worn and the torso must not be included.'

The days dragged on, though Armstrong tried to keep his spirits up. 'Soon I will be on a boat heading for freedom,' he told himself. 'England is just a short distance away.' Then, on 21 January, together with 11 other Allied airmen, and 19 Frenchmen intent on joining the Free French forces in England, Armstrong boarded another fishing boat. In all there were 31 passengers on the 30-foot (9 m) vessel, and just two crewmen. The passengers were squeezed tightly together in the dark of the dank, noisome hold, awash with seawater. Then they had to wait hours for the tide to turn before they could embark. Eventually, half drowned, half suffocated, they felt the boat slip downstream with the tide. Then came a jarring shout of 'Halt!' But the boat did not stop. A searchlight was switched on, and then it was gone. (It later transpired that members of the Resistance on shore had sabotaged its power supply.) The crew started the engine, and then, reaching full throttle, they made a run for it, past the German gun emplacements high above them on the cliffs, out into the open sea. At every moment Armstrong was expecting to hear the shore batteries open fire, but no shots came.

The passage across the Channel was not all plain sailing. A storm got up, the men in the hold were violently sick, and for a while the bilge pump failed to cope and they were taking on water, before the blocked sump could be cleared. But after 18 hours the sea calmed, the crew opened the hatch and the weary men below scrambled out on deck to stretch their cramped, numbed limbs. A new day was breaking, and in the distance they could make out the rugged coast of Cornwall. In a while a Royal Navy patrol boat came out from Falmouth to greet them, and escorted them back to port. 'When at last we set our feet on land,' Armstrong recalls, 'some kissed the ground, others jumped with joy, and all of us, each in his own way, thanked Almighty God for our freedom.'

> Soon I will be on a boat heading for freedom. England is just a short distance away.
>
> James E. Armstrong, *Escape!* (2000)

On his debriefing, Armstrong learnt that two of his crewmen had also made it back to England, via Spain. He himself was repatriated, and after the war studied agriculture at the University of Florida, graduating in 1948. He remained in the US Air Force Reserve, reaching the rank of lieutenant colonel, but in 1961 he began to hear a voice in his head telling him, as he put it, 'There's something more.' Thus he found himself called to the ministry, and until his retirement in 1984 he was pastor of the non-denominational New Covenant Church in Thomasville, Georgia.

Not all those who helped him were so lucky. On 2 February 1944 Yves Le Hénaff, the organizer of the Dahlia Circuit in Quimper, was piloting a motor boat, *Le Jouet des Flots* ('Puppet of the Waves'), carrying 37 men to England when they encountered a storm. The boat sprung a leak and was forced back to Brittany, where Le Hénaff had to beach it on the shore west of Pont-l'Abbé. Three days later he was stopped along with two other Resistance leaders at a German roadblock and arrested. Taken to Paris, he was subjected to lengthy interrogations by the Gestapo, but did not yield a single name. At the beginning of July he was put on board one of the overcrowded 'death trains' destined for Dachau, and at some point during the journey he died. He was not quite 30. Neither the exact date of his death, nor his burial place, are known.

Tragedy on Mont Blanc

The desperate retreat from the Central Pillar of Frêney, 1961

Viewed from the popular tourist town of Chamonix, Mont Blanc, at 15,781 feet (4,810 m) the highest mountain in the Alps, rises gently in a series of snowy dollops. It has grandeur from this northern aspect, certainly, but it is a benign grandeur. It was on this side of the mountain that all the early attempts on the summit were made. In 1783 three guides returned from one such attempt and reported that the only equipment required was an umbrella and a bottle of smelling salts. Three years later the summit was attained; the route taken was little more than a walk – albeit an exhausting one in the thin air.

But on the southern, Italian side, the mountain shows a very different aspect. Here jagged ridges and elegant pillars of red granite soar above a complex of steep, chaotic glaciers, creating a series of savage arenas high above the valley of the Doire. The loftiest of these pillars, the central one of three that rear above the almost inaccessible Frêney Glacier, provides the highest rock climb in western Europe – and, at the time it was first climbed, one of the hardest, culminating as it does in the magnificent, vertical, 500-feet (150 m) spire known as *la Chandelle* – the Candle. Those who aspired to make the first ascent of the Central Pillar of Frêney took with them much more than an umbrella and a bottle of smelling salts: ropes, ice axes, crampons, helmets, slings, hammers, scores of pitons and karabiners, food, stoves and bivouac gear – in the expectation of spending at least a night or two on the mountain.

On 7 July 1961 seven men – three Italians and four Frenchmen – set out to make the first ascent of the Central Pillar, bowed under enormous rucksacks. Only three were to return alive. Recalling the climb and the desperate retreat, one of the survivors, the great mountaineer Walter Bonatti, was to write: 'This is the most tragic story of my life.'

Into the savage arena
Bonatti had tried the route two years previously with his great friend Andrea Oggioni, but the weather had broken. Ever since then he and Oggioni had dreamt of returning. Now they were accompanied by a third climber, Roberto Gallieni. The approach to the route was long and complicated, involving the crossing of a number of difficult, icy cols to reach the remote cirque below the Pillar. The

OPPOSITE The awesome southern flank of Mont Blanc. The Central Pillar of Frêney is in the middle of the dark face that culminates just to the left of the summit. Bonatti and his team approached the Pillar from the right-hand side of the photograph, over a series of cols. They began their descent in a terrible storm from near the top of the Pillar, then down the steep Frêney Glacier directly below the face, and finally over the Innominata Ridge to the left, and thence down to the Gamba Hut. Only three out of seven men made it down alive.

tourists' cable car whisked them several thousand feet up from the valley to the Torino Hut, at the head of the Vallée Blanche. It was late afternoon. From here they traversed across the great snowy bowl between the Tour Ronde and the Aiguilles du Diable – the Devil's Needles – then up a steep couloir of snow and ice to the Col de la Fourche on the Frontier Ridge of Mont Maudit – the Cursed Mountain. Here there is a tiny bivouac hut, lashed onto the rocks of the col with steel cables; and here, inside the hut, Bonatti and his companions found four Frenchmen: Pierre Mazeaud, Antoine Vieille, Pierre Kohlman and Robert Guillaume. It was clear from their piles of equipment that they too had their eye on the Pillar. The Italians offered to back off, as the French were there first. But Mazeaud told Bonatti that he should go ahead, as he had tried the route before. In the end the two teams agreed to join forces.

> 'On these occasions amid the sublimity of Nature's inmost sanctuaries, where no human being has stood before, the mind is capable of asserting itself above the discomforts of the body, and the most prosaic of men will find his thoughts wandering in realms of strange fancies. The forces of the World are vast, and sometimes inexorably cruel; they care little for weaklings; but to those who deliberately set themselves to wrest from them their secrets, they are often kind ...'
>
> Frank Smythe, *Climbs and Ski Runs* (1930), describing the first ascent in 1927 of a 'last great problem' of a previous generation, the *Sentinelle Rouge* route on Mont Blanc's massive Brenva Face

For the next section of the approach to the still-distant Pillar they had to wait for the dead of night, when the temperature would fall well below zero. A hard freeze was essential, as their route was to take them beneath the Brenva Face of Mont Blanc, a 4000-feet (1,200 m) wall of almost Himalayan proportions, which in the heat of the day roars constantly with avalanches. After darkness had fallen and the temperature had plummeted, the seven men rappelled down the other side of the col by torchlight, then made haste to cross the Brenva Glacier before the first beams of the sun began to detonate volleys of ice and rock from the wakening face above. On the far side of the glacier, the ascent to the Col de Peuterey is a long and serious ice climb in its own right, but for Bonatti and his immensely fit companions it was merely a minor passage in their pursuit of the great challenge ahead. From the col, more steep icy slopes took them to the base of the Pillar, at over 13,000 feet (4,000 m). They were now in a very remote position, and about to commit themselves to an even wilder adventure. Burning gold in the early morning light, the Central Pillar of Frêney rose another 2,000 feet (600 m) above them, culminating in the elegant spire of the Chandelle. Beyond the Chandelle they could just make out a thin white line set against the deep blue of the sky. This was the summit ridge of Mont Blanc.

The storm breaks

At first the climb went well. The rock was easier than it looked, and they gained height rapidly. Climbing through till nine o'clock that evening, they reached some small ledges about 1,000 feet (300 m) up. Attached by a cat's cradle of ropes to a piton, they spent the night hunched up, with their feet hanging in space. The cramped position and the bitter cold meant that any snatch of sleep was short-lived, but they were in good heart. They had come a long way in the previous 24 hours, and the clear cold night promised that the good weather would continue. Early the next morning they were greeted by a sight that no one who has witnessed it will ever forget: an Alpine dawn seen from high in the mountains. First a line on the horizon to the east turns from black to blue, then yellow, then orange as the sun breaks above the great mass of Monte Rosa, setting fire to peak after peak across the Western Alps – Castor, Pollux, the Matterhorn, the Dent Blanche, Mont Blanc itself. Despite the blaze of light, this is the coldest time of all. But soon the sun warmed the seven men as they contemplated the challenge ahead.

By midday they were at the base of the Chandelle, at a height of 15,000 feet (4,500 m) – a long way up, a long way out. It was not a place to be if a storm should break – but this is exactly what happened. The wisps of mist that had circled about them as they climbed through the morning now coiled themselves up and unleashed a fury. As if out of nowhere, fierce gusts of wind whipped pellets of snow into their faces so they could not see what they were doing. The cold was piercing, driving into their bones, seemingly determined to chill the life out of them. Even more threatening was the electricity humming in the air.

The alpinist Georges Sonnier left a vivid description of the onset of an electrical storm at the summit of the Dent du Requin in his classic book *Où Règne la Lumière* (1947):

> I felt an unbearable prickling in my finger tips. They started to hum, and my wet rope-soled shoes also hummed. I looked at my companion, his hair was standing on end, drawn towards the sky. I felt my own hair doing the same. Small bluish flames were hovering round us, springing out of the rocks they caressed.

Sonnier managed to escape the lightning strikes by making a rapid descent, but this option was not open to Bonatti and his companions. They took what shelter they could on three cramped ledges. The Italians had a small bivouac tent inside which they could huddle, but the Frenchmen only had waterproof sheets to wrap round their sleeping bags. All their metal equipment – pitons, karabiners, ice axes, crampons – was secured as far away from them as possible, to draw the lighting. Even so, one of the Frenchmen, Kohlman, was hit and almost bowled over into space. For some time he was unable to move his muscles, until Mazeaud administered a dose of the stimulant Coramine.

‘ I had never before been on such a face in such a storm. ’

Walter Bonatti, *On the Heights* (1961)

ABOVE Bonatti's companions prepare the ropes for the descent from the narrow ledge where they spent three nights stormbound high on Mont Blanc's Central Pillar of Frêney.

At first, none of this group of experienced alpinists was too concerned. They had sat out storms before on small ledges, and they only needed the weather to clear for half a day to finish the climb and traverse over the summit of Mont Blanc to the safety of the Vallot Hut, high on the easier northern flanks of the mountain. But – though they did not know it yet – this storm was to continue for days. There was some relief when the thunder and lightning died away into the distance, but the snow continued to fall heavily. Another night passed, the Italians feeling suffocated in their tiny shelter of rubberized cloth, half buried by snow. The dawn seemed to promise a clearing in the weather, and they made ready to launch the final effort to get up the Chandelle. But suddenly the mists returned, and then the wind, and then the snow. Once more they were forced back into their inadequate shelters. Though they could eat, the fierce wind made it impossible to light the stoves, so they could not melt snow to quench their thirsts. Instead they were forced to nibble it in lumps. The condensation inside the tiny tent soaked them to the skin and chilled their bones to the marrow. Another night passed, and still the storm continued.

> Looking back down the jumbled mass of the Frêney Glacier, I began to appreciate the fact that if the weather did turn nasty, a retreat would be a formidable task.

Don Whillans, *Portrait of a Mountaineer* (1971). Whillans, not one given to overstatement, was a member of the team that made the first successful ascent of the Central Pillar of Frêney, less than two months after the disaster.

Climb down through hell

They had left the valley on Sunday afternoon. It was now Friday morning, and the storm had been battering them for 60 hours. Bonatti knew that they did not have the strength left to get up the final 250 feet (60 m) of the Chandelle. They would have to descend.

It was not an inviting prospect. First of all, they must rappel down some 1,500 feet (450 m) of the Pillar. Then there was the steep, broken and dangerously crevassed Frêney Glacier, divided into two sections by a huge ice wall, blocking the narrows between two of Mont Blanc's great ridges, the Innominata and the Peuterey. The only way past was by a series of dangerous rappels down the Rochers Gruber, an area of rotten rock on one side of this formidable obstacle. From there they would have to continue down the glacier, its many crevasses now treacherously concealed by great drifts of snow. Once across the glacier, they would have a difficult climb up to the Col de l'Innominata, before they could at last descend to the safety of the Gamba Hut, 6,500 feet (2,000 m) below where they now clung, high on the Pillar.

With Bonatti in the lead, they began to rappel. Normally climbers thread the doubled ropes they are going to slide down through a cord loop, which is attached to an anchor – a piton or a spike of rock. But in really fierce conditions, fingers are too numbed to tie the double fisherman's knot needed to create the loop, so Bonatti and his team sacrificed a valuable karabiner for each rappel. In the swirling cloud and the falling snow they could not see where they were going, so each time they plunged into the unknown, hoping to find a ledge before the rope ran out. At one point Bonatti found himself at the end of the rope, with no ledge in sight. Despite the wind he managed to make himself heard, and his companions lowered another rope. After all seven of them had slid down the rope to the next ledge, they had to pull the ropes down – hard work with the ropes now so stiff and ice-encrusted – before setting up the next rappel. Even with the extended rope, Bonatti at one point found himself nowhere near a ledge, and had to make a series of pendulum swings to reach one, where he could hammer in a piton. So it went on, rappel after weary rappel, for 12 hours, until they reached the foot of the Pillar and the upper section of the Frêney Glacier. It was late in the afternoon.

They waded down through the snow, sometimes plunging up to their chests, looking for a place to shelter for the night. The wind still howled, the snow still fell. That evening they finished the last of their food. Kohlman's condition was deteriorating, and his fingers were showing the first signs of frostbite. Bonatti gave him the

> We were desperate, but no one said a word. Finally, Oggioni said to me: "Let's make a vow: if we get out of this safely, let us forget that the Pillar even exists." I said: "Yes."
>
> Walter Bonatti, *On the Heights* (1961)

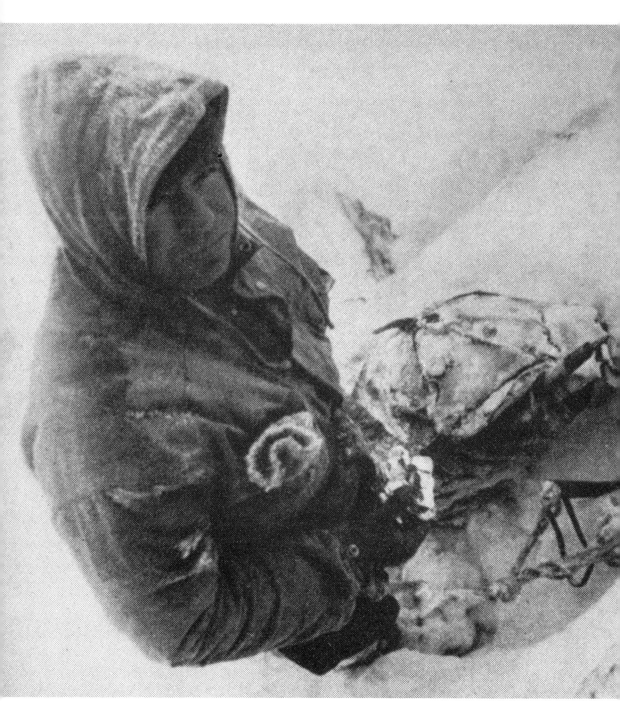

ABOVE Two years before the Central Pillar climb, Bonatti and Andrea Oggioni (pictured here) made the first ascent of another high and difficult climb on Mont Blanc's south face: the Red Pillar of Brouillard. Oggioni was to perish on the descent from the Central Pillar.

bottle of cooking alcohol to rub onto his livid skin, but Kohlman, already distracted, swigged a couple of mouthfuls of the poisonous liquid before the bottle could be seized from his hands.

The morning brought no change in the weather. All attached to a single rope, they ploughed a furrow through the deep snow – exhausting work even for those who are physically fresh. At the same time there was the constant anxiety that the whole slope would avalanche, sending them to certain death over the great ice wall below. Vieille was at the end of his tether. Every step or so he would collapse, only to heave himself up again somehow, urged on by his companions. At last they reached the top of the Rochers Gruber, and Bonatti embarked on the first rappel, followed by Kohlman. When after a time none of the others had appeared, Bonatti climbed back up to see what was happening. 'Vieille is dying,' he was told. And then, on the snow, he could make out the body of Vieille, attached by a length of rope to a rock. His companions had wrapped him up in the bivouac tent. They could not bear to think of his flesh being pecked at by the crows.

At last, by the middle of the afternoon, they had reached the foot of the Rochers Gruber. Bonatti had thought he had heard voices below him, but the snow on the glacier was pristine when they reached it; no rescue parties had come looking for them. Their mood of dark despair deepened even further, but they pressed on down

THE FIRST ASCENT

AT THE END OF AUGUST 1961, fully aware of the tragedy that had unfolded only the month before, the British climbers Don Whillans, Chris Bonnington and Ian Clough, with the Polish mountaineer Jan Djuglosz, set their sights on making the first ascent of the Central Pillar. Hot on their heels was a French party led by René Desmaison. All the way up the Pillar they came across signs of the desperate retreat: new karabiners hanging from rappel anchors, ropes dangling down the face. Then, on reaching a ledge near the foot of the Chandelle, they found piles of abandoned gear. Above, there were numerous pitons battered into the cracks, sometimes only inserted a quarter of an inch, sometimes bent and mangled. It was a sign of the desperation of Bonatti and his companions. After a cold bivouac, they set off again, this time into the complete unknown. It was a daunting prospect, as Whillans himself described:

> There was no doubt as to what had stopped previous attempts. For at least 500 ft, a monolithic candle of rock rose vertically to the sky. A crack split the tower for the first 80 feet or so and then – as far as I could see – there was nothing.

At one point Whillans found himself dangling from a hold above 2,000 feet (600 m) of space, with his strength running out. Eventually he could hold on no longer and fell – only to be held by the rope. Eventually they made it to the top of the Chandelle, and headed for the summit of Mont Blanc. There they were greeted by a French journalist, who offered them a bottle of wine. He'd kept it chilled for them in the snow.

the glacier, negotiating the mazes of crevasses as best they could. Oggioni, who had done sterling work bringing up the rear, helping his weaker companions, was now on the verge of collapse. Gallieni took his rucksack. Guillaume was even weaker, and sat down in the snow. He could go no further.

Bonatti led the way up towards the Col de l'Innominata. Another thunderstorm was approaching, the route was iced up, it was impossible to find a place to hammer in a piton. They were now so weak they were barely making any progress. Oggioni was fading fast, and Bonatti decided to leave him with Mazeaud, the strongest of the French team, while he and Gallieni would take Kohlman with them and make what speed they could to the Gamba Hut, where they could summon a rescue.

At this point, Kohlman's mind finally snapped. He slid down on his back, threatening to drag the others with him to their deaths. He was delirious, raving, waving his hands about, suddenly possessed of almost demonic energy. He charged in a fury first at Gallieni, then at Bonatti. They could only keep him at bay by pulling the rope – Kohlman was tied to the middle – in different directions. Eventually the two Italians managed to free themselves from the rope and rushed down the slopes towards the Gamba.

It was three o'clock on Sunday morning when they reached the hut. They hammered on the windows to wake those within. Soon a rescue party was organized, while Bonatti and Gallieni were given hot drinks and dry clothes before falling into a deep sleep. Some hours later the rescuers returned. Only Mazeaud came down with them. The others – Vieille, Guillaume, Kohlman, Bonatti's dear friend Andrea Oggioni – were all dead.

It was one of the worst tragedies, not only in Bonatti's life, but in the entire history of alpinism.

THE INESCAPABLE ROCK

ROCK

The last victims of Alcatraz, 1962

Small, remote and preferably barren islands have long been favoured as places of incarceration – especially for those whom the state wishes to rot away. In ancient Rome the Emperor Augustus, outraged at reports of the sexual excesses of his daughter Julia, exiled her to the island of Pandataria to ponder on her sins. Mary Queen of Scots, another woman accused of harlotry, was confined on Castle Island in the middle of Loch Leven, while Napoleon, the bogeyman of Europe's *anciens régimes*, ended his life on the remote South Atlantic outpost of St Helena. For centuries the rocky Château d'If in the Bay of Marseille served the French as a prison for religious and political dissidents (and the fictional Count of Monte Cristo), until they discovered Devil's Island off the coast of French Guiana. But perhaps looming largest in the popular imagination is Alcatraz, 'the island of the pelicans', a rock-girt lump in San Francisco Bay from where no man ever escaped and lived to tell the tale.

The US military started to build fortifications on Alcatraz in the 1850s, to defend the great natural harbour of San Francisco Bay. During the Civil War 'the Rock', as it is known locally, became an internment camp for Confederate sympathizers. In the 1870s, as an official military prison, it was used to hold a group of Hopi Native Americans, then prisoners taken during the 1898 war with Spain. During the First World War conscientious objectors were imprisoned on Alcatraz in appalling conditions, leading one inmate to describe the place as 'Uncle Sam's Devil's Island'.

The resort of desperate men

In 1934 Alcatraz became a federal penitentiary for America's most hardened and recidivist criminals. Among its more notable inmates were Al Capone and Robert Franklin Stroud – misleadingly dubbed 'the Birdman of Alcatraz' (see box p 172). During the 29 years of its existence as a penitentiary there were more than a dozen escape attempts by some three dozen prisoners, but all those involved were either drowned, shot dead or recaptured. The first man to die was Joe Bowers, who in April 1936 was shot while trying to climb over a chain-link fence and fell over the cliff to his death on the rocky shore below. In December of the following year two prisoners managed to make it into the waters of the Bay, but there was a storm running, and it is assumed that they were swept out to sea by strong currents. Even in summer the

UNCLE SAM'S DEVIL'S ISLAND

THE ANARCHIST PHILIP GROSSER wrote a pamphlet with this title in the 1920s about his experiences on Alcatraz, where he was held during and after the First World War for his anti-militarist beliefs. Despite his conscientious objection to the draft in 1917, he was forcibly inducted into the army, and thus subjected to its harsh discipline. During his three years on Alcatraz he refused to wear army uniform, stand in formation or break rocks, and as a consequence was subjected to an array of cruel and unusual punishments: he was beaten, dragged around on a rope, and constrained upright in a 'coffin cage' measuring only 23 inches (57 cm) wide by 12 inches (30 cm) deep. Following his release Grosser became increasingly ground down by poverty, and took his own life in 1933. After his death his friend, the physician Harry Block, wrote that his pamphlet on Alcatraz would always be timely: 'The dogs of war are still mad, and unleashed.'

waters of the Bay are cold, no more than 50–55 °F (10–12 °C), quickly sapping a man's strength and will to live. The prison authorities prevented the inmates from becoming acclimatized to cold water by making sure the water in the showers was always hot.

The bloodiest attempt at a breakout was the so-called 'Battle of Alcatraz' in May 1946, when six prisoners took a number of guards hostage. The authorities called in the Marines, who deployed tactics perfected during the Pacific War against entrenched Japanese positions. Two guards and three prisoners were killed in the fighting, and afterwards a further two prisoners were executed in the gas chamber. The only escape attempt that came close to success took place in 1962, the year before the prison was closed for good. It was a carefully planned, cleverly executed operation, which subsequently became the subject of a film, *Escape from Alcatraz*, starring Clint Eastwood as Frank Morris, the mastermind behind the escape. But none of the three men who made it out and launched a raft into the dark waters of the Bay on the night of 11 June 1962 were ever seen again.

Drills, dummies and raincoat rafts

Frank Morris had spent much of his life behind bars. As a child he'd been placed in a series of foster homes, and was convicted of his first crime at the age of 13, subsequently advancing to felonies such as narcotic possession and armed robbery. It was his penchant for escaping that had resulted in his transfer to Alcatraz in January 1960, where he became prisoner number AZ-1441. By the following year, Morris had begun to work out an escape scheme, and invited two brothers, John and Clarence Anglin, also armed robbers, and the occupant of the cell next to his, a car thief called Allen West, to join him.

They began by scraping away at the vent holes in their respective cells, using a variety of crude implements, including spoons, nail clippers, some old saw

THE BIRDMAN OF ALCATRAZ

WHILE IN PRISON THE DOUBLE MURDERER ROBERT FRANKLIN STROUD became famous as a world authority on the diseases of birds, based on studies of the numerous pet canaries that he kept in his cell. In 1962 he became the subject of a fictionalized film, *The Birdman of Alcatraz*, starring Burt Lancaster in the title role. The title is misleading, however, as all of Stroud's scientific work had been carried out at Leavenworth Prison in Kansas, before his transfer in 1942 to Alcatraz, where he was not allowed to keep birds. In 1959 Stroud was transferred again, this time to a prison hospital in Springfield, Missouri. Here he died, still incarcerated, in 1963, having spent 54 years in prison, 42 of them in solitary confinement.

blades that West found while on a cleaning detail, and an improvised drill. The first motor for the drill came from a pair of barber's clippers, but this could not provide sufficient power. By a stroke of luck, the guards asked West to fix a broken vacuum cleaner, which it turned out had a spare electric motor. Having fixed the main motor, he was able to 'borrow' the spare for the drill without anybody noticing. The four men undertook their excavation work during evening music hour, so the noise of their scraping was partly muffled – but the drill proved too noisy, and not very efficient, and was abandoned. Every night they would conceal their work by filling the holes with old newspapers mushed up into a paste. Once they had chipped their way out, they were able to start work on a vent in the ceiling of the corridor that gave access to the roof.

Another part of the plan was to make dummy heads to protrude from the blankets on their beds, so that a cursory night-time inspection would reassure the guards that all was well. To make the heads they used cement powder mixed with soap and toilet paper. Skin tone was added using paint from the prison's art kits, and the barbershop provided the human hair to top off the effect. The final part of the plan, for the final part of the escape, was the creation of a raft and lifejackets, patched together with glue from some 50 raincoats handed over (voluntarily or unknowingly) by other inmates. The raft – which measured 6 feet by 14 feet (1.8 by 4.25 m), and which also incorporated barrels and wire mesh – was to be inflated using an adapted concertina.

By 11 June 1962 the men had breached the top vent. Unfortunately for West – or perhaps fortunately – he had been unable to complete the removal of the vent in his cell, and despite Clarence Anglin's attempt to kick it in he was stuck. The others decided to go for it without him. They wriggled some 30 feet (9 m) up the flue to the roof, from where they shinned down a 50-foot (15 m) drainpipe to the ground. Sometime later West succeeded in breaking through his cell vent, and made his way to the roof. But the others had long gone – and no more was ever heard of them.

Did they make it?

West despondently returned to his cell, and in his subsequent interviews with the authorities he outlined the remainder of the escape plan. The raft was to take them to Angel Island, from where they'd swim across the Raccoon Strait to the mainland of Marin County. Here they were to steal a car, raid a men's outfitters to obtain civilian clothes and then go their separate ways.

ABOVE Frank Morris, the mastermind behind the 1962 breakout.

Despite speculation that Morris and the Anglins had broken Alactraz's record for inescapability, the FBI, after lengthy investigations, concluded that they had died in the attempt. There were no records of car thefts or burglaries at men's outfitters in Marin during the relevant time. The men had no connections with wealthy mobsters who might have picked them up in a launch, and their families did not have the financial resources for such an escapade – the men were completely on their own. Although their bodies were never found, that is not unusual in San Francisco Bay, where the drowned are often swept out to sea under the Golden Gate Bridge. However, various items belonging to the men were found the day after the escape, including one of the homemade lifejackets with heavy teeth marks on the mouthpiece, indicating a desperate struggle to blow air into it and stay afloat.

On 17 July 1962 the crew of a Norwegian ship sailing some 20 miles (32 km) northwest of the Golden Gate spotted in the distance a body floating face down in the water. Through binoculars, the corpse could be seen to be wearing denim trousers similar to those issued to prison inmates. No other missing person from the period had been reported as wearing such clothes.

No one will ever know for sure whether Morris and the Anglins were in fact successful in getting off the Rock alive. But they never contacted their families, so it is safe to assume that Alcatraz maintained its reputation for inescapability to the end of its days as a federal penitentiary.

The prison was closed the year after the escape attempt, the authorities citing the expense of running the place, the erosion of the buildings by salt water, and the pollution of the Bay by sewage produced by prisoners and staff alike. In 1986 Alcatraz was designated a National Historic Landmark, and continues to be a popular destination with tourists looking for a frisson of the Rock's dark past amidst its grim, deserted buildings.

The Spy who went over the Wall

Soviet double-agent George Blake
escapes from Wormwood Scrubs, 1966

George Blake was one of the Soviet Union's most effective double-agents, said by Dick White, then the head of MI6, to have inflicted more damage than the notorious traitor Kim Philby, the 'Third Man' of the Cambridge Spy Ring. When Blake was eventually caught in 1961 he was sentenced to 42 years in prison – then the longest sentence ever handed down by a British court. The judge described his case as 'one of the worst that can be envisaged in times of peace', although the details of the damage he caused remain classified. It is thought he may have betrayed as many as several hundred British agents.

In 1966 Blake made a dramatic breakout from Wormwood Scrubs Prison in London, and such was the professionalism of the escape that it was widely thought that the KGB, or the IRA, or even the British intelligence services themselves, must be responsible. It was to be another 22 years before the truth came out.

The making of a double-agent

Blake came from a cosmopolitan background. His father, Albert Behar, was a Spanish Jew who had lived for many years in Cairo, and who, as a naturalized British citizen, had fought against the Turks during the First World War. After the war Behar settled in the Netherlands, where he met and married Blake's mother. Blake was born in 1922. After his father's death in 1936 he was sent to live with his father's sister in Cairo, and here he was exposed to the communist beliefs of his older cousin. At that time, Blake had ideas of becoming a minister in the Dutch Reformed Church, but his cousin planted a seed that was to bear fruit many years later. Blake was back in the Netherlands when the Second World War broke out, and after the German invasion of May 1940 he obtained false papers and worked for the Dutch Resistance. In 1942, disguised as a monk, he escaped to Britain, where he joined the Royal Navy. It was at this point that he adopted the name Blake. He was soon transferred to intelligence work because of his language skills, and part of his job was to escort agents into Nazi-occupied Holland.

After the war, Blake was recruited by MI6, Britain's Secret Intelligence Service, and in 1948 he was sent to Seoul, the capital of South Korea, under cover as British vice-consul. When North Korea invaded in 1950, Blake and other

---

Western diplomats were captured and interned in the North. Here he read the works of Karl Marx, but it was what he witnessed during the Korean War that underlay his conversion to communism:

> It was the relentless bombing of small Korean villages by enormous American Flying Fortresses. Women and children and old people, because the young men were in the army. We might have been victims ourselves. It made me feel ashamed of belonging to these overpowering, technically superior countries fighting against what seemed to me defenceless people. I felt I was on the wrong side ... that it would be better for humanity if the Communist system prevailed, that it would put an end to war.

Of course, at the time he kept these views to himself, and on his release at the end of the Korean War he resumed his work for MI6, which then posted him to Berlin in order to recruit Soviet double-agents. Unbeknownst to his controllers in London, he made contact directly with the KGB, and offered to work for them.

A decent human response

Blake was eventually exposed by a Polish defector, and in April 1961 was recalled to London from Beirut, where he was attending an Arabic course. The government was deeply embarrassed, and tried to persuade Dick White, head of MI6, to bury the affair. MI6 refused to cooperate, but all the same Blake's trial was held in camera. The maximum sentence for a breach of the Official Secrets Act in peacetime was 14 years, but the judge sentenced him to 14 years on each of three counts of spying, to run consecutively. As it turned out, Blake only served five of the 42 years.

> ‘I could have left the service, and I could have joined the Communist Party, and I could have sold the *Daily Worker* at street corners ... But I felt I could do more for the cause.’
>
> George Blake, interviewed on Russian TV, 2007

In 1970 Sean Bourke, an Irish Republican who had been in jail with Blake, revealed his role in Blake's escape, but it was only in 1988 that two radical peace activists and self-styled 'quasi-anarchists', Michael Randle and Pat Pottle, revealed that it was they who had masterminded the affair. They were, they said, outraged at the 'vicious' and 'unjust' sentence passed down on Blake, and that 'helping him was a decent human response'. They had themselves served 18 months in Wormwood Scrubs after organizing demonstrations outside a US Air Force base in Essex in 1962, and it was during this time that they befriended Blake and Bourke. They rejected Blake's suggestion that they contact the Soviet embassy for assistance in their escape plans, as they regarded the Soviet Union as inimical to their own ideas of liberty. 'It was,' Randle said, 'to be an entirely unprofessional – almost one could say DIY – affair.'

ABOVE George Blake relaxing with his mother in the Carpathian Mountains in September 1967, the year after his escape to the Soviet Union.

An entirely unprofessional affair

Randle and Pottle kept up contact with Blake by means of a smuggled walkie-talkie radio. The breakout was planned for an early Saturday evening, when most of the prisoners and guards would be watching a film. Blake had already loosened two panes of glass and the bar that divided them in the great Gothic window at the end of his landing, and using a wooden frame in his cell had practised squeezing through a gap measuring only 12 by 18 inches (30 by 45 cm). When the appointed time came, he unfixed the tape holding the loosened panes and bar in place, wriggled through the gap and dropped down to the ground. Meanwhile, Bourke had parked a getaway car close by, and then threw an improvised rope ladder, with rungs made from size-13 knitting needles, over the prison's perimeter wall. Blake scrambled up before he could be spotted, and dropped 20 feet (6 m) down the other side, breaking his wrist in the process.

Bourke drove Blake to a safe house nearby, where the idea was that Blake should disguise himself as an Arab (he had perfected the language in prison) in order to get out of the country. To this end, he was to take large doses of meladinin, a drug used to treat the rare disease called vitiligo, characterized by the appearance of pale patches on the skin. The idea was that the drug would darken his skin to a Mediterranean hue, but Blake refused to take it, fearing the serious side effects. The false passport they had been hoping for also failed to materialize, so in the end Randle and Pottle decided to smuggle Blake out of the country in a specially adapted camper van. Thus in December 1966 Michael Randle and his unwitting family arrived in East Berlin in the camper van, ostensibly for a holiday, with Blake concealed in a specially constructed secret compartment.

From East Berlin, Blake was spirited off to Moscow, where he was made a colonel in the KGB and awarded the Order of Lenin. He worked at the Institute for World, Economic and International Affairs, divorced his first wife, by whom he had had three children, and remarried. On his 85th birthday in 2007, as Anglo-Russian relations began to deteriorate to Cold War levels of chilliness following the murder in London of dissident former-spy Alexander Litvinenko, President Putin awarded Blake the Order of Friendship. 'It is hard to overrate the importance of the information received through Blake,' said Sergei Ivanov, spokesman for the SVR, successor to the KGB's foreign-intelligence arm. 'It is thanks to Blake that the Soviet Union avoided very serious military and political damage which the United States and Great Britain could have inflicted on it.' At the award ceremony, Blake said that he had had a 'very full and, in the end, a happy life'. The agents he betrayed might have put it rather differently, if they had still been alive.

> 'The Communist ideal is too high to achieve ... and there can only be nominal adherents to it in the end. But I am optimistic, that in time, and it may take thousands of years, that humanity will come to the viewpoint that it would be better to live in a Communist society where people were really equal.'
>
> George Blake, quoted in the *Independent*, 1 October 2006

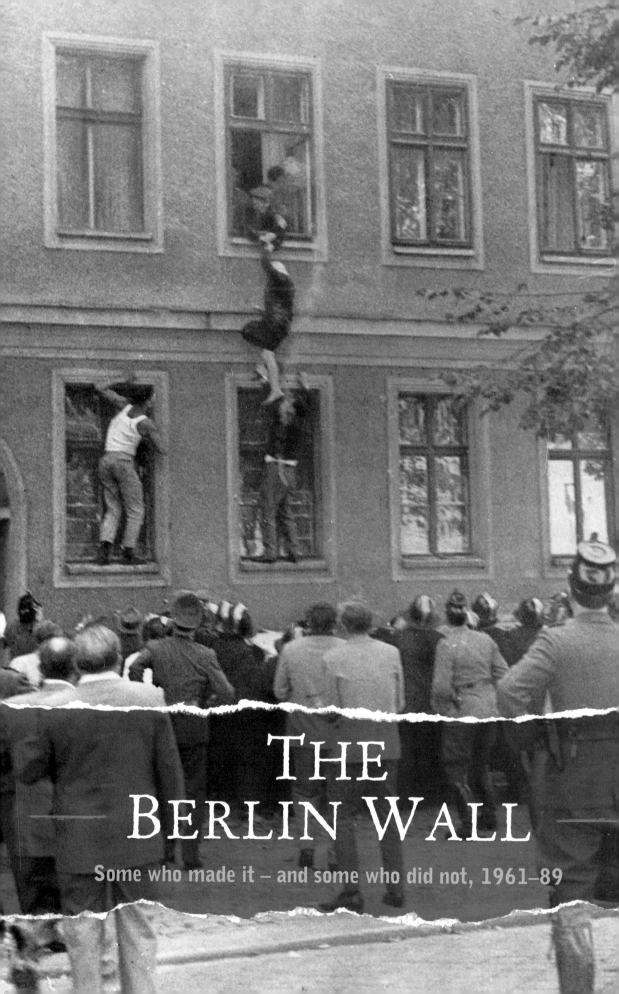

THE
BERLIN WALL

Some who made it – and some who did not, 1961–89

In the early hours of 13 August 1961 a Warsaw Pact communiqué was issued from Moscow. 'In the face of the aggressive aspirations of the reactionary forces of West Germany and its NATO allies,' it read, 'the Warsaw Pact proposes reliable safeguards and effective control be established around the whole territory of West Berlin.' In the morning, Berliners woke up to find work had begun on a barrier of barbed wire and concrete that for three decades was to separate the Soviet zone in the east of the city from West Berlin, that little island of democracy in the midst of the communist bloc. The response of the USA was muted: President Kennedy, accepting the realities of an ideologically polarized world, commented, 'A wall is a hell of a lot better than a war.'

The unstated aim of the 'Anti-Fascist Protection Wall' was not to keep Western armies out of East Berlin, but to stem the flood of East Germans seeking a better life in the West. Some 200,000 a year were leaving, including many highly trained professionals, scientists, technicians and skilled workers, many of them young men and women. This haemorrhage was threatening the future of the young socialist state: 'If the present situation of open borders remains,' Walter Ulbricht, the East German president, had warned Moscow in July 1961, 'collapse is inevitable.' A Communist Party pamphlet produced in 1955 had already stated that 'leaving the GDR [German Democratic Republic, i.e. East Germany] is an act of political and moral backwardness and depravity', that going to work for West

> ‘ No one has the intention of building a wall. ’
>
> President Walter Ulbricht of East Germany, in *Neues Deutschland*, 17 June 1961

German 'factory owners and militarists' was a betrayal of 'what our people have created through common labour'. But even after the construction of the Wall, the lure of political freedom – and shops full of consumer goods – proved too strong for many to resist. Until the Wall came down at the end of 1989, thousands of East Germans managed to escape across it, some by great feats of ingenuity. Tragically, at least 136 – possibly as many as 200 – would-be escapers died in the attempt.

OPPOSITE 22 August 1961: 77-year-old Frieda Schulze escapes from the ledge of her East Berlin apartment window, which overlooked West Berlin. While an East German policeman holds her from above, a West Berliner pulls at her ankles. Eventually she dropped into the blankets held out by the West Berlin fire brigade.

The Wall is reinforced

The initial somewhat ad hoc barbed-wire fence with its sections of concrete, brick and rubble proved vulnerable in places to lorries driven at speed. One escape party customized a low-level sports car so that the windshield and roof would come off when it was driven under a steel barrier at Checkpoint Charlie, one of the main official crossing points. Various anti-vehicle devices and zig-zagging approach roads soon put paid to such high-speed escapes.

In June 1962 a second, parallel barrier was erected some 100 yards (90 m) within East German territory. All buildings between the two barriers were demolished, so giving the border guards in the watchtowers an uninterrupted view and a clear field of fire. The ground in the so-called Death Strip was covered in raked gravel, so any footprints would be clearly seen. In 1965 the original barrier was replaced with a 12-foot (3.5 m) high concrete wall; this in turn was replaced by an even stronger structure in 1975.

'The measures taken by our government serve to protect democratic Berlin and its people. They are an effective blow against the illegal, subversive smuggling of human beings organized by the extremists in Bonn [capital of West Germany]. This means that the security bodies have the task of preventing the citizens of our Republic and its capital being made into victims of unscrupulous slave traders. This entails preventing the entry of our citizens into West Berlin.'

Statement by the government of the GDR issued on 14 August 1961

One of the first to make it across the Wall was an East German soldier, Hans Conrad Schumann. On 15 August 1961, two days after the barrier went up, he had been guarding the barbed-wire fence, every now and then pushing down the top of the wire, when a young man approached on the Western side. 'Get back immediately!' Schumann shouted. But then he whispered, 'I am going to make a run for it.' The young man alerted the West Berlin police, and when their minibus stopped for a moment, as if on routine patrol, Schumann abandoned his post and jumped over the barbed-wire entanglement, discarding his gun as he ran.

The first barrier proved insufficient to stop many escapees on foot. Not all of them made it, however. One victim, 21-year-old Gerhard Kayser, was spotted in the early hours of 27 October 1961 entangled in the barbed wire. He had been shot. The East German border guards then dragged his body back, and he later died in hospital. Many more were to die in this fashion, some of them in the glare of the world's press (see 'A very public death', p.184).

ABOVE A memorial to the many victims who died attempting to cross the Berlin Wall.

Running, jumping, swimming, tunnelling

At first, despite the barrier, there were many ways to cross over to the West. A number of apartment blocks abutted the barrier, and, although any doorways on the border side were bricked up, people could jump out of upper-storey windows. Some dropped down notes for the West Berlin police, who would arrange for the fire brigade to spread out their blankets to catch jumpers. On 22 August 1961 58-year-old Ida Siekmann threw down a mattress from the third floor of her building, but when she jumped after it she missed. She was the first person to die at the Wall. Shortly afterwards, a 77-year-old woman called Frieda Schulze was standing fearfully on her window ledge, contemplating jumping into the fire brigade's blanket below, when she was seized from behind by an East German policeman. She managed to wriggle off the ledge so that the policeman was holding her whole weight, while two men from the crowd of West Berliners below jumped up and grabbed her ankles. The elderly lady was eventually pulled down into the blanket. Subsequently, the windows of these buildings were also bricked up, and by the end of September the authorities had begun to vacate all the residents in the apartment blocks abutting the barrier.

Within a week of the building of the Wall, Easterners had found that they could get under it by crawling through the municipal sewers. A rainwater drain running from East to West, accessible by lifting a grating, proved particularly popular – in one night alone 28 people made it across – until the gratings were replaced with manhole covers secured with bolts. Where there were no existing subterranean routes available, people sometimes made their own. With the help of his friends, a West Berliner, Peter Scholz, dug a 60-foot (18 m) tunnel 9 feet (2.5 m) under the Wall to

A VERY PUBLIC DEATH

AT 2.15 IN THE AFTERNOON OF 17 AUGUST 1962, Peter Fechter, an 18-year-old bricklayer, and another teenager, Helmut Kulbeik, made a dash for it across the Death Strip. They were spotted by the border guards, and a total of 35 shots rang out. Kulbeik scrambled over the barrier, but Fechter was hit in the back or the pelvis, and fell, fatally wounded, at the foot of the Wall. On the far side, police and US soldiers quickly appeared on the scene, soon joined by photographers and a crowd of angry West Berliners. From a nearby observation platform Fechter's body could be seen, crumpled up into a foetal position, a pool of blood spreading out across the ground. 'Why don't you help me?' he called out. The American soldiers could do nothing but throw over a medical kit, but Fechter. as he slowly bled to death, was too weak to make any use of it. Eventually, under cover of tear gas, a group of East German border guards dragged him back. He was bundled into a car and taken to hospital, where he died at 3.15 p.m.

rescue his fiancée and their baby, together with nine others. It was slow, dangerous work, with the constant worry that the roof would cave in, or that the slightest noise might be detected by the patrols above their heads. The baby was sedated to prevent it from betraying them with a cry, and dragged behind them in a metal basin pulled by a rope. On another occasion, two tunnels were being dug so close to each other – unbeknownst to the respective tunnellers – that the ground in between subsided, giving the game away. Siegfried Noffke, a young Westerner who was hoping to get his wife and child out, was shot dead.

> ' Do not hesitate to use firearms, even when the border breakouts involve women and children, a ruse that the traitors have already frequently used. '
>
> Order issued to East German border guards, 1 October 1973, by the Stasi, the secret police

Berlin's canals and rivers, the Spree and the Havel, where they coincided with the border, also provided an escape route. In the first week a number of people swam across the Teltow Canal, risking the bullets of the border guards – who had standing orders to shoot to kill any 'traitors' trying to escape. On the afternoon of 24 August Gunter Litwin, a 24-year-old tailor, was not so lucky: when he attempted to swim the Humboldt Canal he was shot. Five days later another young man, Roland Hoff, sank in the Teltow Canal after he was hit by a hail of bullets. More swimmers were to meet the same fate; others simply drowned. But in September 1961 a young married couple made it across the Havel, pulling their 18-month-old infant behind them in a bathtub.

The Wall comes down

The escapes, and the killings, continued through the 1960s, the 1970s and the 1980s. With the advent of Mikhail Gorbachev as the new Soviet leader in 1985, a change began to come about. As well as instituting liberalizing reforms at home in the USSR, Gorbachev made it clear that he would not intervene to prevent reform in the Soviet satellite states of Eastern Europe. The leadership of East Germany, however, was one of the most conservative of all the Eastern Bloc regimes, and General Secretary Erich Honecker told his colleagues that he would 'never allow here what is happening in the Soviet Union'. Even as late as January 1989 he declared: 'The Wall will still be standing in fifty or a hundred years if the reasons for its existence are not removed.'

Shortly after Honecker made this statement, just before midnight on 5 February 1989, a waiter called Chris Gueffroy, who wanted to open a restaurant in the West, crossed the inner barrier and the Death Strip and reached to within a few metres of the Wall when he was shot through the heart. He was the last person to die at the Wall. A month later, on 8 March, Winfried Freudenberg took off from the East in a homemade balloon. He successfully crossed the border, but something went horribly wrong over the Western district of Zehlendorf, and he plunged from a great

'The Wall will still be standing in fifty or a hundred years if the reasons for its existence are not removed.'

Erich Honecker, general secretary of the Socialist Unity Party (the East German Communist Party), made this statement inJanuary 1989, just ten months before the Wall came down

height down to his death. No one knows the identity of the last person to die: he was a youth, aged around 18, who drowned on 16 April 1989.

That summer Hungary – one of the more liberal of the Eastern Bloc states – opened its border with Austria. Tens of thousands of East Germans set off to holiday in Hungary, and then slipped over the Austrian border, and on into West Germany. At home the East German regime was faced with mass demonstrations, and on 18 October Honecker resigned. More and more East Germans were leaving, now via Czechoslovakia, and the chaos was such that on 9 November the new East German leader, Egon Krenz, announced that people would be allowed, with the correct permission, to travel directly from East to West Germany, and that all crossing points, including those in Berlin, would be open. This was intended to take effect the following day, but once the announcement had been made tens of thousands of East Berliners flooded to the checkpoints. The border guards had received no instructions, and faced with the impatient crowds they lifted the barriers. It was the end of three decades in which the Wall had separated father from daughter, mother from son, husband from wife, friend from friend, three decades in which the Wall had symbolized the tense and dehumanizing impasse of the Cold War. Now the Wall became a quarry for souvenir hunters, the 'woodpeckers' who came with their hammers to chip off fragments of concrete. By the time that East and West Germany had been formally reunited in October 1990, the Wall had all but been dismantled. Today you can trace the line where the Wall once stood, and peer into the cold waters of the rivers and canals where so many were shot or drowned. But, apart from short stretches preserved as a historic monument, all that remains to remind you of the brutal aberration that was the Berlin Wall are the scattered memorials to those who died.

Author's Acknowledgements

In writing this book I have drawn upon a wide range of sources. In particular I would like to acknowledge the following:

Albert, Paul, 'An Anarchist on Devil's Island', *Black Flag Quarterly*, Vol. 7, No. 5, Winter 1984, reprinted in the *Bulletin of the Kate Sharpley Library*, No. 13, December 1997

Anon., '1966: The Blake Prison Escape', libcom.org

Anon., 'The Great Escape from Alcatraz', www.alcatrazhistory.com

Armstrong, James E., *Escape!* (Honoribus Press, Spartanburg, N.C., 2000)

Benuzzi, Felice, *No Picnic on Mount Kenya* (E.P. Dutton, New York, 1953)

Bonatti, Walter, *On the Heights* (Nicola Zanichelli S.p.A., Bologna, 1961; English translation by Lovett F. Edwards, Ruper Hart-Davis Ltd, London, 1964, reprinted by Diadem, 1979)

Brandon, Ruth, *The Life and Many Deaths of Harry Houdini* (Martin Secker and Warburg, London, 1993)

Bray, Elizabeth, *The Discovery of the Hebrides: Voyagers to the Western Isles 1745–1883* (Collins, Glasgow, 1986)

Bray, John, 'My Escape from Richmond', *Harper's New Monthly Magazine*, April 1864

Bretholz, Leo, and Olesker, Michael, *Leap into Darkness: Seven Years on the Run in Nazi Europe* (Constable, London, 1999)

Brooks, Richard, *Cassell's Battlefields of Britain and Ireland* (Weidenfeld & Nicolson, London, 2005)

Campbell, Roy (translator), *The Poems of St John of the Cross* (Harvill Press, London, 1951)

Carroll, Tim, *The Great Escapers* (Mainstream, Edinburgh, 2004)

Casanova, Giacomo, *The Memoirs of Jacques Casanova de Seingalt* ('The rare unabridged London edition of 1894 translated by Arthur Machen to which has been added the chapters discovered by Arthur Symons')

Daunton, Claire, 'Edith Cavell', *Dictionary of National Biography* online

Dear, Ian, *Escape and Evasion: Prisoner of War Breakouts and the Routes to Safety in World War Two* (Arms and Armour Press, London, 1997)

Defoe, Daniel, *The History of the Remarkable Life of John Sheppard, Containing a Particular Account of His Many Robberies and Escapes* (John Appleby, London, 1724)

Fraser, Antonia, *King Charles II* (Weidenfeld & Nicolson, London, 1979)

Fraser, Antonia, *Mary Queen of Scots* (Weidenfeld & Nicolson, London, 1969)

Goodare, Julian, 'Mary [Queen of Scots]', *Dictionary of National Biography* online

Guy, John, *My Heart is My Own: The Life of Mary Queen of Scots* (Fourth Estate, London, 2004)

Halpin, Tony, 'Vladimir Putin honours traitor George Blake with tit-for-tat birthday medal', *The Times*, 14 November 2007

Harrer, Heinrich, *Beyond Seven Years in Tibet: My life before, during and after* (trans. Tim Carruthers, Labyrynth Press, South Yarra, Victoria, Australia, 2007)

Herrick, Claire E.J., 'William Brydon', *Dictionary of National Biography* online

Hilton, Christopher, *The Wall: The People's Story* (Sutton, Stroud, Gloucestershire, 2001)

Irvine, Ian, 'George Blake: I spy a British traitor', *Independent* online, 1 October 2006

James, Ian, 'Notorious French Prison Turns Into a No-Man's Land', *Los Angeles Times*, 15 December 2002

Jeffries, Lionel, 'The Great Escape Caused Maximum Disruption', *Australians at War*, www.australiansatwar.gov.au

Kavanaugh, Kieran, and Rodriguez, Otilio (translators), *Collected Works of St John of the Cross*, revised edition (1991)

Kearney, Peg Goggin, '"They Die in Youth And Their Life is Among the Unclean": The Life and Death of Elizabeth Emerson' (University of Southern Maine, 1994, http://wprokasy.myweb.uga.edu/Emerson2.htm)

Kelly, Ian, Casanova: *Actor, Spy, Lover, Priest* (Hodder & Stoughton, London, 2008)

Linklater, Eric, *The Prince in the Heather: The Story of Bonnie Prince Charlie's Escape* (Hodder and Stoughton, London, 1965)

Lynch, Jack (ed.), *The Complete Newgate Calendar*, at http://andromeda.rutgers.edu/~jlynch/Texts/sheppard.html

Mackenzie, S.P., *The Colditz Myth: British and Commonwealth Prisoners of War in Nazi Germany* (Oxford University Press, Oxford, 2004)

March, Jenny, *Cassell's Dictionary of Classical Mythology* (Cassell & Co, London, 1998)

Mather, Cotton, *Magnalia Christi Americana; or The Ecclesiastical History of New-England* (1702)

McCoog, Thomas M., 'John Gerard', *Dictionary of National Biography* online

Moore OCDS, Thomas, 'Our Lady and Saint John of the Cross', www.ourgardenofcarmel.org

Nichol, John, and Rennell, Tony, *Home Run: Escape from Nazi Europe* (Viking, London, 2007)

Regan, Geoffrey, *The Guinness Book of Military Blunders* (Guinness, Enfield, Middlesex, 1991)

Rengers, Christopher, *The 33 Doctors of the Church* (TAN Books, Rockford, Illinois, 2002)

Rollings, Charles, *Prisoner of War: Voices from Captivity during the Second World War* (Ebury Press, London, 2007)

Rottman, Gordon L., *The Berlin Wall and the Intra-German Border 1961–89* (Osprey, Oxford, 2008)

Schofield, Hugh, 'Papillon is alive and well in a Paris retirement home', *Mail & Guardian* (South Africa), 26 June 2005

Sebag-Montefiore, Hugh, *Dunkirk: Fight to the Last Man* (Viking, London, 2006)

Sonnier, Georges, *Où Règne la Lumière* (Albin Michel, 1947)

Still, William, *The Underground Railroad* (Porter & Coates, Philadelphia, 1872)

Tripp, Edward, *Crowell's Handbook of Classical Mythology* (Thomas Y. Crowell, New York, 1970)

Whillans, Don, and Ormerod, Alick, *Don Whillans: Portrait of a Mountaineer* (Heinemann, London, 1971)

Whitford, Kathryn, 'Hannah Dustin: The Judgement of History', www.hawthorneinsalem.org

Williams, Eric, *The Wooden Horse* (London, 1949)

In addition, I would like to thank the following: Richard Milbank, my publisher at Quercus, for commissioning the book; Emma Heyworth-Dunn, managing editor at Quercus, for overseeing the book through to press; Victoria Huxley and Geoffrey Smith of Windrush Publishing Services for editing and layout; and the staff of Hornsey Library, for their continuing and cheerful willingness to dig out forgotten volumes for me from the reserve collection.

Index

Index

Index

Index

Quercus
21 Bloomsbury Square
London
WC1A 2NS

First published in Great Britain in 2009

A CIP catalogue record for this book is available from the British Library

ISBN-13: 978-1-84724-682-0

Printed and bound in China

10 9 8 7 6 5 4 3 2 1

Picture Credits

The publishers would like to thank the following for permission to reproduce illustrations:

Alamy.com: pages 129,137,175; Bridgeman Art Library: pages 8, 10-11, 15, 23, 25, 30, 43, 50-1, 53, 60, 65, 87, 91,100, 102, 104, 106, 169, 183; Corbis: pages 76, 81, 89, 95, 120, 126; Getty Images: pages 35, 109, 144, 152, 156, 173, 178; John Cleare, www.mountaincamera.com: page 160; Mary Evans Picture Library: pages 63, 83; National Archives UK: page 158; Steve Le Bell, www.asweepingview.com: page 37; Topfoto: pages 74 (The Granger Collection/Topfoto), 114, 116, 133, 135, 149, 180. Photographs on pages 164 and 166 are scanned from *On the Heights* by Walter Bonatti © Nicola Zanichelli 1961.